Dangerously Different

Lisa T. Storr

WESTBOW
PRESS®
A DIVISION OF THOMAS NELSON
& ZONDERVAN

Scripture quotations taken from the Amplified® Bible (AMP), Copyright © 2015 by The Lockman Foundation. Used by permission. www.Lockman.org

WestBow Press books may be ordered through booksellers or by contacting:

WestBow Press
A Division of Thomas Nelson & Zondervan
1663 Liberty Drive
Bloomington, IN 47403
www.westbowpress.com
1 (866) 928-1240

ISBN: 978-1-9736-6053-8 (sc)
ISBN: 978-1-9736-6054-5 (hc)
ISBN: 978-1-9736-6052-1 (e)

Library of Congress Control Number: 2019904645

Print information available on the last page.

WestBow Press rev. date: 05/17/2019

Chris and Devin

There is not enough room on this sheet of paper to describe the limitless love I have for both of you. The confident men who continuously shower me with unconditional love, unsolicited encouragement, and insurmountable support assure me that I am blessed way beyond what I deserve. This foundation is what brings me comfort as I continue walking out my most difficult assignment from God: the role of being your mother. I know it has not always been easy, but that is a mere indication of the level of favor God has bestowed upon us. As we continue trusting God in our journeys, separately and together, I know our best is truly ahead of us.

Love you guys real hard!!

Mom

#LURH

Contents

chapter 1

God

Unscheduled breakouts of tears, the seesawing emotional clues that let me know my life belongs to someone other than myself, occupy my soul. For years I have attempted to quiet the powerful voice that pulls me toward a peculiar place and threatens my interpretation not only of God but also of myself. In His current position in my life, there is no real threat, because my presence with God is minimal and very much filtered. This is mostly due to my lack of trust and understanding of His love and grace toward me. Nonetheless, the brawl within intensifies into an overpowering wrath. The clash could be ascribed to my resistance to halting the erroneous contributions I continue making into this counterfeit, selfish, unfocused life. The power struggle is so incredibly real that the fight obstructs me from striding toward the great future that is only available through Christ. The pressure entangling my emotions consumes my thoughts, so the only question I am fixated on at the moment is this: could it really be possible that I, Lisa Therez Storr, am dangerously designed by God himself?

Having to face the solicited response is difficult. After all, in the balance, it's awkward to think of oneself as being dangerously designed. But the truth remains that I *am* dangerously designed by the hands of God, even though, at times, it is difficult for me to accept. However, once I embraced this revelation, my new life began to take shape, and growth toward purpose emerged. It wasn't easy, because more often than I care to admit I questioned whether God could truly love someone like me. Keep in mind I am fully aware of my untold story. I have lived long enough to experience some great highlights, some tedious low points, and those routine, mundane moments that are impossible to forget. Yet I wasn't prepared to openly share all the unattractive details of my life with God at this time. It's comical how I was acting—as if God were clueless about my past.

Even more laughable was the fact that, despite my conflicting actions, I still wanted to continue in the chase. The more I questioned God's love for me, the more He allowed understanding to flow throughout the depths of my heart until I fully grasped the fact that His love toward me will never waver.

Despite my struggles, I found out that God truly does love me unconditionally. It was particularly noticeable during those early life-development stages when I was not walking in His will for my life. I discovered God does not base His love for me on my performance, my being perfect, my appearance, or all the mistakes I have made. He knows my beginning, my in-between, and my ending, so nothing I have done or will do comes as a surprise to Him.

Thank God for His mercy and faithfulness toward me. This certainty of His love toward me is the foundation of my relationship with Him today. As I scrutinized my life in my late thirties, I realized that I had never fully made God my number one priority or lived up to my responsibility in our partnership. Some would say I was merely a limited partner; I was only partially invested. I believed that going to church, paying my tithes, attending Sunday school, and knowing the politically correct Christian lingo meant I was doing my part in the arrangement. Boy, was I way off base! I allowed doubt and insecurities to govern my belief system. I never completely committed to God or to His promises, because I really didn't believe it was possible for me - especially not with my background. However, this was just an attempt to justify my unbelief. I lacked confidence in His abilities for me, even though I had no problem believing it was possible for others. I was a hypocrite.

I excluded myself from being fully devoted to God because there was an absence of intimacy in our relationship. I was experimenting with God, not experiencing God. How do I know this? Gazing through the rearview mirror of my life, many of my actions and responses were calculated to dodge hurt, rejection, humiliation, neglect, isolation, and failure. More importantly, with my limited, inadequate concept of God, I was constantly forfeiting opportunities to experience the giving and receiving of authentic love in most of my relationships due to my envisioning the worst outcome. I fell short in my ability to allow the authentic Lisa to be visible—even to myself. That is, until one day, when I was in my mid to late thirties, and everything changed as I stood in my laundry room.

I remember the incident as clearly as if it were yesterday. I can still see myself standing in this small, dry, isolated space crying uncontrollably, with tears rolling down my face. I was unable to put the pain I was feeling into words. I didn't just cry;

I wept until every ounce of the agony that was contaminating my soul could be overheard. The only escape or discharge from my frantic sobbing was my deep wailing out to God. I begged Him profusely to release the intense pressures that had unexpectedly found their way into my life, infecting and polluting my very existence. I needed - and was determined - for God to show me how to live the Jeremiah 29:11 life that I had heard believers describe in exquisite words. But never in my own life had I consistently experienced any portion of this magnificent, splendid life.

During this time, I was not in a healthy, stable, or balanced place in my journey. I was bleeding internally. As judgment sneaked in, I had to admit that in previously unfavorable times I was emotionally driven to seek God as if He were my very own sugar daddy. I had persuaded myself that I could manipulate God with my erratic, unpredictable, dramatic responses with such passion that the academy award would go to me, Lisa Storr. I thought my actions would motivate God to immediately deploy perfect solutions on my behalf to fight for my cause. Please don't be mistaken. I am extremely aware of all my phony prayer requests whereby I literally tried to bargain with God about my petty, undisciplined, self-seeking desires. My memories of those actions have not been erased; instead, I see them now as impressionable, teachable lessons that drew me closer to God, so I could be purified, and our relationship could be restored.

However, on this ordinary Sunday morning, that proved not to be the case as I tried to compel God to deal with my problems. I wasn't looking for a quick fix; I wanted a real cure for my condition. I'm not sure how or when it happened, but some extraordinary insight of love purged my soul and made that moment distinctly different from all the others. This time, my outburst wasn't because I was seeking a man or tangible blessings like money, a new house, or an expensive car. Quite the opposite. I required something much more vital from God, and it could not be seen by the naked eye.

I needed more than a touch. I needed to be able to rest in His presence as I submerged in His anointing. My heart, the navigation system of my life, was shattered, crushed, and defective. It was in desperate need of a complete overhaul by the hand of the Master, if I were to have any chance of living to see another day. I not only needed God's help, but His help was mandatory for my survival. I was afraid, I was alone, and I was desperate. My children, the emotional shopping sprees, the tropical vacations, food, and even my high-powered career were no solace for the grief that was consuming me. No; I was discovering this process I was engaging in was dispatched on purpose. There was no exit clause that would allow me to remove myself from the process and remain in His will. The pressure was designed to provoke me to see and accept that I was indeed the chosen candidate to accomplish this exclusive plan orchestrated by God. His training methods are brutal, but they are meant to improve my skills and qualifications to produce great results for His kingdom. It is also worth noting that they are the only permissible instructions I could undergo to claim His blessings and certify that I am indeed the trusted recipient of such a great promise.

This process established God as my only true source and revealed that everything else was simply a resource. This series of events was being used to clarify the areas of concern that needed to be addressed if I was going to outlive this season of my life and secure God's plan for my future. I couldn't turn away now. I had come too far in the preparation process to settle for merely being acquainted with destiny.

The on-the-job training challenged me to see if I would implement the knowledge I acquired from the Word into my daily lifestyle. There is a huge difference between comprehending God's Word and applying God's Word to your own personal life. I did the research and found out the positive implications of having a local church in my life. This study forced me to try to discover why it is imperative to fellowship with other believers, regardless of previous negative church experiences. It also provided me with an incredible amount of wisdom to equip me to distinguish the correct path that would guide me toward purpose. While all this was going on, I was given an unanticipated amount of courage that was essential for me to complete my tasks.

It was incredible how I fell so madly in love with God during this period of my life, which had appeared so bleak and hopeless. The pain my broken heart had suffered did not equate to the love produced by God during the renovation of my heart.

It is indescribable how my heart was restored, refreshed, and revived after this process. I was alive again. I didn't want to pretend that I didn't care when people hurt me, or that things didn't bother me when I felt like I was doing the work and no results could be seen. I wanted to be open, honest and vulnerable. I was finally in a position to receive completely from God and I was not about to waste time on nonsense. My decisions and my actions were now in sync. I was one hundred percent invested in my relationship with God. This was the pivotal moment that transformed me; I let go of my will and the ill will I felt towards all the people who had treated me unjustly. Instead of harping on the past, I used my energy to start speaking words of power to my future. These words of power – "I am nothing without Him, and with Him all things are possible", greatly influenced my transition by silencing all the negativity competing for my attention. As my faith was maturing, my vision became clearer, and I saw the enormity of God. My dependency on worldly artifacts took a direct hit as I shifted my dependency to God. As Christ kept calling me, Hebrews 12:6-11 Amplified Bible (AMP) helped to change my perception of myself. As I read the words "for the Lord disciplines and corrects those whom He loves, and He punishes every son whom He receives and welcomes [to His heart]", I found rest and insight with my previous struggles with God. The words uncovered that even though I see myself as unworthy, God values me. I started seeking out scriptures that supported how God sees me to help improve my self-image. I had on-going, positive self-talks because I understood the power of the words I say about myself. Every day I would recite words that increased my faith, renewed my mindset and expanded my vision. In my bathroom mirror, I would look at myself and declare what God says about me no matter how I may have been feeling on any given day. Scriptures such as "I am the head and not the tail", "I am above and not beneath", "I am a lender and not a borrower", "I am of a royal priesthood and I am fearfully and wonderfully made" were the stimulation I needed to stay grounded as I continued pursuing God by faith. I have learned (and I am still learning) how not to be easily offended, because I am now aware that I am not the one personally under attack. Therefore, I am making the necessary adjustments so that I do not take it personally. I recognize that the offenses from others often have nothing to do with me, Lisa the person. The wrongdoing is against the sovereign God whose light shines through me. In those human moments when life happens - and it most certainly will - none of us are exempt. I must purpose in my heart to avoid being drawn to do what is familiar, comfortable and ineffective. I am learning how not to second-guess purpose or my value as I forge ahead, trusting that the plans for my life will work out for my good. I understand that I must be diligent at residing in a state of forgiveness and in total awareness of who I am and who I represent. It's an ongoing battle risking the God in me to a world that glamorizes people and things of little or no substance. It is between this rock and hard place that my best praises have erupted. In this place, I have learned that God hid me until I was mature enough to carry out His vision. He was determined not to be guilty of giving the world too many opportunities to be captivated by the imitation me. Once I could be trusted, His endorsement was all that I would ever need to thrive. This was the ammunition I needed to reinforce my responsibility and authority over this life that I once took for granted.

Armed with this new-found strength and truth, I qualified for my next assignment. Fear and failure no longer controlled my thoughts or actions. The influence of the safeguarded, defensive, chaotic heart I once idolized was diminished. No longer aspiring to abuse the gift of life that God loaned to me, I made a conscious vow to love myself completely and honestly. I became secure in my source of strength, the Holy Spirit. God was equipping me with His wisdom to handle whatever came my way. This all-encompassing godly mental power is a weapon

I never want to live without. It directs my heart to freely give God's love to all within my spheres of influence. This technique thrust me into a position where purpose was achievable. For the first time in a very long time, I have that peace that everyone talks about which passes all understanding. I could sense that advancement was on the horizon. What was being concealed, the area of my life that would be most affected. However, what was being revealed, it would require a great sacrifice. When you are in the right position and your heart is pure, it doesn't take God long to start unfolding the plot.

To say I didn't see it coming in this form is an understatement. I was lying in bed shortly after having breast surgery when God revealed the highlights of His plan to me. I was abruptly awakened from the effects of the medications I had taken prior to leaving the hospital. I am sure the four individuals sitting in my bedroom at the time assumed that my tears were from the severe pain that was consuming my body, but this was far from the truth. I was sobbing intensely because in that moment there was no doubt in my mind how much God truly loves me, with a love so deep that I know without a shadow of a doubt I do not deserve it. Yet He continuously offers it to me at no charge. His capacity to love without holding back is unbelievable. Don't let me get off track because it doesn't take much, especially when I think about how His love has changed me. I can break out into a praise dance and forget everything.

As I surveyed the room, I noted that not everyone there was biologically related to me. Yet on that Monday morning they all laid aside every one of their own personal lives to support and take care of me. It was an incredibly overwhelming feeling to be amid such compassion. There are no words to express the confusion I felt. Gasping for air as I relived this memory, the tears began to roll. God looked past my massive mistakes and reached down from Heaven to touch the hearts of so many people just to let me know how much He cares for and values me. At first it was difficult for me to accept God's ability to love me to this magnitude when there were times in life when I didn't even acknowledge Him publicly for fear of being treated as an outcast. Yet all that was visible in this moment was the residue of God's mercy in refusing to inflict the punishment I knew I deserved for the way I regarded him. Somehow, my physical pain no longer mattered because my spirit was demanding my attention - but not without a fight.

There is a constant tug of war against pride trying to control my motives. Independence has its drawbacks. This superiority complex attempts to deceive me into believing that asking for help undermines my independence and makes me appear weak. This argument is quite convincing because, for years I struggled with asking for assistance, even from those closest to me. Perhaps it was due to my intense reluctance to show vulnerability and humility or to be viewed as a burden. I had a difficult time accepting the assistance offered, so I constantly repeated familiar behavior habits. Countless times I made excuses as to why it would be impossible for someone to provide me with support. I thought about the other person's work schedule and their family responsibilities until I talked myself right out of asking for their assistance. The sad part was that the mental anguish I put myself through was simply a deflection to avoid being rejected. I'm not sure if the inability to take care of myself physically inspired the sequence of events that projected a light on my deficiency. However, for a person who has always been extremely self-sufficient, this reality scared me. Whatever the case, it all proved far too strenuous for me to handle.

What I didn't understand at the time was that God was birthing something great and new within me. On that day I conceived a little company known as Love You Real Hard Inc., and I had no idea how to strategically cultivate that assignment. However, God continuously uses Love You Real Hard a/k/a LURH as a platform for me to extend unconditional love to those who feel they are undeserving, just like I once did. It is more apparent to me now that my life thus far has been one gigantic lesson to prepare me to align me with that destiny, if I chose that path. The process, far from ideal, gave me the confidence and courage I needed to let purpose have its way. My conscious decision to bring my efforts in line with God's will did not offer immediate rewards. At times, my heart grew heavy and the days seemed extremely long, especially in an age in which instant gratification is prevalent. It took some time for God to work out the kinks in me. Being in a place of vulnerability, as depression is yearning for your attention, took determination for me to defeat. No one ever thinks about the high cost associated with accomplishing destiny and reaching purpose. We are naive to the level of trust that is the prerequisite for this type of service unto the Lord. To attain this kind of status, I underwent extended periods of suffering and isolation that required me to demonstrate an attitude of joy throughout the injustice. While under fire, as my mustard sized seed of faith to move mountains was being challenged, I had to remind myself that a good man's steps are ordered by the Lord.

As I unraveled, pride started losing the control it once had over my life. I discovered there is an extremely thin line between pride and being prideful. To prevent falling prey to the effects of pride in the future, I chose to replace it with being thankful and grateful in all things. These conditions sound feasible, until the variables of real life do not support the direction God is taking you. I had to be careful not to become obsessed with the "lights, camera, action" without concentrating on what happens behind the scenes before the curtain is raised. I had to be willing to abort what worked for me in the past -familiarity and comfortability - for my relationship with God to flourish. Being comfortable and accepting the familiar were natural responses for me. Normalcy and routine required little or no faith and added very little change to my life. Plus, those efforts were counterproductive. I had to fully surrender and let humility freely flow as pride was released from its reign, in order for my relationship with God to blossom. At the end of the renovation process, God is in His rightful position in my life. This act sealed the deal. He occupies the highest place of honor, where He is my EVERYTHING!

Now when I wake up I am so thankful, because this one detectable act of allowing His breath to flow through my body is truly a gift of significance. It is a constant reminder of His great love, compassion and faithfulness, that can be seen in the authentic Lisa. As I open my eyes every day, gratefulness overtakes my soul as God confirms there is purpose for Lisa in this day. Through the process, I have been given the ability to hear His voice ever so clearly. By actively listening, my awareness to the needs of others has increased. Those are the opportunities in which the fruit of His Spirit must be visible. My life must reflect one of noble character, exhibiting love, joy, peace, patience, kindness, goodness, faithfulness, gentleness, and **self-control to continue this journey.** His truth is evident and produces such profound clarity in my life. Even when life attempts to discredit my actions, I rely on His faithfulness and His assurance of my value. I am ever so grateful that He has allowed me to live long enough to see Him supply my needs according to His riches and glory. As I recap the times He has been my provider, my healer, my way maker, the one that sticks closer to me than a brother, and my keeper, all the chaos that once tried to disqualify me is somehow overshadowed. I am indebted to Him for continuing the chase until my original worth was restored. I now have the confidence that in my advancement to the next level of learning how to love the authentic Lisa, I will win. It is a journey during which, I am sure, I will discover how to love God in ways that will result in my receiving His presence continually. Keep seeking that friend request from Jesus, the one you weren't expecting, hit 'confirm" and buckle up for the greatest ride of your life.

chapter 2

Me

What much is given, much is required! I was hit by a car when I was in my mother's womb, and then again as a child, while chasing after my older brother Dino, who was regrettably killed at the unfortunate and early age of forty-two. I was uprooted from everything familiar to a foreign land, I was injured in a grease fire as a teenager, I became an unwed mother and had multiple failed marriages, and I suffered illnesses that led to five major surgeries. This was my life and the world labeled me as flawed, inadequate, unusable and ineffective. The irony and unfortunate part about these remarks was that I too bought into the world's opinion of me. Yet, through all my pitfalls and difficulties, I am overwhelmingly blessed - far beyond what I could have imagined because God Himself established me as valuable. Long before I ever understood my worth, He put His stamp of approval on me. When I was nameless and anonymous to the world, He chose to anoint me for greatness. While others may consider me flawed, God's designer label declares that I am a favored, loved, anointed, and a dangerous woman equipped for destiny. Well, perhaps I *am* flawed. However, the visualization of a woman with such impeccable qualities frightens me to my core. Why, do you ask? It is because when I secretly allow the meaning of these excellent qualities to tiptoe around my soul which is not often, my mind instantaneously travels back to my unrighteous past, where the scars I try to conceal continue to threaten my potential growth towards purpose. As the tears freely flow, I can hear in my mind the words leaping out of the book of Romans. My attention gravitates towards chapter 8, mainly at verse 28: "...and you know that all things work together for the good of those who love him, who have been called according to His purpose." Internally, there is a war brewing as I am being challenged by my current predicament. By no stretch of the imagination does it indicate that anything in my present condition is working for my good, yet, I am intrigued as to how these words can one day become my absolute truth.

It is in this atmosphere and in similar moods that I recant how very little I truly understood about the power of God's love. That is, until I unbolted the locks surrounding my overly suspicious and guarded heart and allowed myself to engage with Proverbs 3:5 Amplified Bible (AMP): "Trust in and rely confidently on the Lord with all your heart and do not rely on your own insight or understanding." As the verse penetrates deep within my spirit, I can only equate it to the specialized environment needed for a plant to develop its roots. As the word begins to take shape, I can see myself becoming anchored; of course, not without dispute. Unbelief shows up in the backdrop fighting to catch my attention, offering opposing options for me to try, even though they do not yield any substantial, lasting results. Yet, the doubting part of me indulges in the thought that they may be worth at least a stab; after all, how else can I find out if something really works? This distraction makes me aware that this will not be an unchallenged fight. There will be no overnight success story in the cards for me. So, as you can probably foresee, some time had to pass before my will was surrendered. However, once I was fully convinced and accepted this revelation as my truth, the worry and concern subsided. Trusting in a physically untouchable God became plausible as the aftermath of untrusting people who had once hurt me started to lose its salty edge. I had to remind myself of the importance of my adapting this principle to see real change transpire within me. The understanding of this passage in Proverbs made it attainable. It gave way for my faith to throw caution to the wind, trust in the Lord with all my heart, and not depend on my own limited human comprehension on certain issues that often led me down the path of unnecessary distress. Despite these awakenings, this process was still quite difficult, especially since my more established apprehensions were a tad bit more complicated. I could be unreasonable when it came to accepting information that could not be intellectually explained, or when asked to invest in the process of trusting people when the benefits were hidden. As soon as I started making a little progress, my mind would drift back to some of my various unhealthy choices that would only increase my hesitation to believe and to continue moving forward. This uneasy feeling, which resulted from placing far too much trust in people who lacked appreciation for its value, left me feeling powerless. That was something I had no desire to repeat; nor was I eager to revisit it. Those lessons took my mind to a dark place, where the pain I endured was much more visible than the lessons I learned. Thank God for His word. Even though I tried to avoid these types of intimate Jesus moments like a death sentence, more extensive studies were necessary. Through these probes, I unintentionally discovered that my lack of trust in others was strangely related to my inability to completely trust God in all things. It wasn't obvious to me at the time that my relentless, unhealthy state of mind was the driving force slowing down my healing process. My many setbacks were hindering me from following the pathway designed by God that would allow me to prosper. Thank God those same distractions that could have caused my demise were no match for my destiny. So, to say the least, I am extremely grateful for my will being overruled.

It took the infiltration of Romans 8:38-39 Amplified Bible (AMP) to sustain my connection with God to where I now have no doubt that He is my number one priority. This portion of scripture assures me that I am convinced [and continue to be convinced beyond any doubt] that neither death, nor life, nor angels, nor principalities, nor things present *and* threatening, nor things to come, nor powers, nor height, nor depth, nor any other created thing, will be able to separate us from the [unlimited] love of God, which is in Christ Jesus our Lord.

It saddens me to know that up until my late thirties I was truly unaware of the magnitude of God's love for me or the extent of my value. His love is so unbelievably powerful, that I am constantly baffled by how He freely and unconditionally He chooses to offer it to "little ole me". Thank God for the freed mindset that opened the portal for me to accept God's love while embracing self-forgiveness. I teasingly chuckle to and at myself because if the process was the length of my two previous thoughts, I would have excelled early at this thing called "life".

However, my reality was quite different. The process almost crushed and consumed me simultaneously.

Sometimes, the day-to-day effort required for survival was too difficult for me to conjure up. It made more sense to return to what was familiar, because it appeared to be an easier route to follow. But God had a different plan for my life. He introduced me to His Holy Spirit to help me when circumstances seemed overwhelming. Through the guidance of the Holy Spirit I learned how to quit reasoning with all the "what ifs" of life that might happen. God dealt with me in the places where I felt unsafe. He showed me how to decipher my insecurities and overcome the resistance I believed disqualified me from greatness. Slowly, but deliberately, the emotional walls of my past began to fall. He disabled the power that was attempting to delay my progress. The problems that came from my being an unwed mother, a divorcee, a depressed woman, a single parent, and a financially unstable woman were being removed. He tore down every dominating force that tried to suffocate His plan for my life. The path that God intended for me to live was available, and all He needed was an absolute "yes" from me. From God's repairing of my cracked foundation, I learned to acknowledge my past and let it go, giving myself permission to move on and let happiness bloom again.

By saying yes, I denounced every other route that provided no guarantees or assurances; methods that simply had me going around in circles like a gerbil on a wheel. Instead, I chose to use every ounce of the faith I had cultivated as my incentive to believe in my "yes" to God. My listening skills are being developed to clearly recognize the voice of God throughout my journey. Little by little, the unbelief and doubt that fight against my sense of purpose are being defeated.

For a short time, I permitted myself to rewind my past decisions and imagine how one different choice could have changed the woman that I am now; the woman who now has a healthy lifestyle filled with gratefulness and unconditional love. Yet, at the same time, I hesitate to even explore this theory, knowing that one minor adjustment could have completely shattered the outcome that I believe is imperative for my legacy. While I do appreciate their efforts to bring some form of clarity, those flashbacks are truly unnecessary now. The clarification I desired has been granted, letting me know that if any alternative route had been selected other that the path that knitted my will with the will of God, the outcome of my life would have been very different. Additionally, this assignment is what challenged me to learn how to unconditionally love the authentic Lisa which is one of the most difficult things I have ever had to do, but indispensable for the success of my journey.

For as long as I can remember, I was too ashamed, embarrassed and insecure to allow the real Lisa to have a public presence. The result was that I isolated parts of myself due to my fears. I was overloaded with all kinds of emotions, wondering what people would think if the authentic Lisa was exposed. When one is seeking external validation, this is a risk not worth seizing. I was constantly measuring my flaws by the standards of the rest of the world, and so my focus was easily redirected to those minor periods that now lack relevance to my future. Lisa's representative worked diligently to steal the forefront from the authentic Lisa. Sporadically, the authentic

Lisa could be seen participating in my malfunctioning life, but only on an as-needed basis. The drawback of this scenario was that God required much more of the original *me*. He wanted His creation of me to no longer go unnoticed. He wanted my life to shine. He wanted the *me* that is openly willing to worship Him to stand up. He wanted the *me* that is thankful to be seen, regardless of the condition of my life. He wanted the *me* that daily seeks to live a life of holiness to be visible. The *me* that understands that it is better to be obedient than to have to offer up a sacrifice. The *me* that is both willing to give and receive unconditional love. The *me* that would be faithful to Him amid chaos. The *me* that would be willing to fellowship with others without a self-centered worldly approach. He no longer wanted the authentic *me* to remain silent in the background. Good news; at the same time God was sending out His requests, I was exhausted, had very little fight left in me, and desperately wanted emotional, financial, physical and spiritual relief. So, in my weakness, when I became completely unguarded, God's strength prevailed. It took a great deal of work, time and effort to release all the pinned-up emotions I was concealing. The picture of how much He sacrifices for me is imbedded within my soul: how could I possibly entertain the idea of declining such an offer from God? I fought hard to discipline myself to disregard every diversion to reclaim my rightful position in God. I learned how to guard, strengthen, and renew my mind because this is where all the battles kick off. I embraced the fact that in some fights I will suffer losses. However, my efforts were primarily geared toward winning the internal war of my mind, not every encountered confrontation. In His Presence,

He provided a safe place of refuge for me to cry and to express my anguish, sadness, hurt and guilt without interruption or judgment. He listened as I shared my feelings about my own imperfections and damaging decisions. When I was rebellious, He reprimanded me in ways that made me want to be better. As a listener, He made the environment conducive for me to reveal how those same actions affected me as a person and impacted those whom I so deeply love. He paid full attention when I had no words that corresponded with what was arising in the lowest part of my soul. He gave me permission to rest when the distress of the pain was insurmountable, and my burdens felt unbearable. And just like that, in a twinkle of an eye, the universal attributes of a loving father who wants only what is best for His children are present and available. His love gently guides me towards the place where I uncovered the courage to love and accept myself. It is a love without reservation.

During this process, He found ways to bless me beyond my expectations. But what I am most mindful of is the way His kindness, His faithfulness, His love, His patience and His mercy were all accessible to me, who, by all merits, didn't deserve any of them. His love is such a powerful inspiration; still, because, like most of us I confused the counterfeit with the real for so long, I was alarmed. After all, I was one of the people who was convinced that one hundred percent commitment to anyone or anything eventually leads to heartache, betrayal and deficiency. This inaccurate information governed most of my adult life relationships. However, over time, I did finally and totally commit myself to God and His plan for my life because I saw myself through the eyes of Christ. The image is indescribable until you read 1st Peter 2:9 Amplified Bible (AMP):

"..but you are a chosen race, a royal priesthood, a consecrated nation, a [special] people for God's own possession, so that you may proclaim the excellencies [the wonderful deeds and virtues and perfections] of Him who called you out of darkness into His marvelous light." It is an excellent passage of scripture that commands how we should view ourselves as believers. *Knowing* who you are is only a portion of the battle. *Believing* who you are is the wisdom needed to live a victorious life. I am comforted to know that in some ways my past inadequacies and untimely mistakes prepared me to do the required work to obtain my great future. My previous historical actions do not define the woman I am today. By doing the essential work on self, God had room to freely share His good news in and through me. The benefit to me is that He continuously opens the windows of heaven and pours out blessings in the places of my life that were once toxic. Then He seamlessly dropped my company, Love You Real Hard, Inc., into my spirit.

At first, I must admit I was intimidated that God selected me to steer the Love You Real Hard movement - a movement so intertwined with my purpose that God Himself positioned me to be its pilot. This undertaking of showing unconditional love to others is massive, and the responsibility is intensely way above my pay grade. However, because I am called for such a great assignment, the rewards are limitless. This journey continually affords me daily opportunities to make a difference in the lives of those who lost hope, just like I did. If our shared experiences connects us to the Almighty God, I know I must be walking in purpose. Through faith, I believe that this love mission will manifest globally, because the God I serve only deals in the impossible, where someone like me can receive the incredible. Check out John 10:10 Amplified Bible (AMP). "The thief comes only in order to steal and kill and destroy. I came that they may have *and* enjoy life, and have it in abundance [to the full, till it overflows]." Now that's love!

chapter 3

Purpose

Starting somewhere around my early twenties, individuals with whom I had little to no interaction would approach me and nonchalantly tell me how God was going to use me to change the game and that it was going to be great. In other words, they saw a great call on my life. The confidence with which they described the visions floating around in their brains was mind-blowing, especially since I secretly assumed God only revealed such things *about* me *to* me. Of course, their words sparked my curiosity and I wanted to know more; not from all of them, just from the ones who appeared to be genuine. Part of me was also intrigued by how some of the things they said registered with me and were so uncomfortably accurate. Others, on the other hand, were so out in left field that I speculated as to whether they really did have a relationship with God, especially because of their eagerness to prove the genuineness of their relationship with God. On the other hand, the ones with whom some form of connection could be felt caused something to resonate within my spirit that drew me closer towards the direction of God. I am certain this was due to their demonstration of boldness and power when they interjected the name of Jesus, although parts of me believe this form of undertaking was mainly used for my benefit, in order to validate the exchange. However, what most of them failed to consider was how their methods puzzled me. They gave off the impression of being a bit abrasive and overly forceful, which was somewhat extreme for my liking. This was basically because, at this stage of my life, their techniques didn't make complete sense to me, and their behavior was somewhat intense. Still, the human side of me felt compelled to examine the agitating information they shared voluntarily. I am sure part of what was troubling me was how some of their insights oddly resembled imaginings of equivalent meaning to me. Those memories heightened by sensitivity radar.

Looking back on those occurrences, I now know why I felt so unsettled. It was due to my greenness regarding the prophetic ministry and of myself rather than the individuals sharing information. Most of my hesitation to embrace this belief system was due to my lack of awareness. It bothered me when I couldn't determine why strangers found it necessary to share information about me, with me, when they had no idea who I was. Sadly, I was going through an identity crisis and didn't even know it. I had not yet fully discovered the effects of the released power of God that led to my transformation from unhealthy to healthy. I had yet to realize that being uncomfortable is not always a bad thing. It can often be that little sign of reassurance letting you know that you are on the right path. Instead, I let my insecurities dictate the uneasy feelings I felt when faced with these types of parameters. I would internally question whether it was due to my physical disposition, or whether it was because they had just eavesdropped on my private conversations or watched me engage with people nearby before approaching me. As I tossed all these options around in my head, I concluded that they just might be the individuals God used to bring the clarity and the confirmation I needed to hear in order to move forward. Whatever their reasoning, such revelations, when uttered by unsolicited strangers, were mystifying to me. Reliving these kinds of uninvited moments is delicate for me to handle even today. It reminds me of a time when attending church left an unpleasant feeling in my heart. Don't get me wrong; I wasn't always this hard-hearted towards church. I enjoyed attending church and experiencing all of the things associated with being a part of something greater than myself. As a child, church was fun and safe. The people responsible for my well-being cared about me. The community of God-fearing believers provided stability so that I could learn and ask questions to strengthen my faith walk. All this was possible through their acts of love and godly guidance; that is, until my early adulthood, when I was unfairly treated by members of the body of believers lacking godly character.

For years I had heard how the church is a hospital for the spiritually sick; not just any kind of a hospital, but one that offers a wide range of care for every imaginable spiritual ailment. A place where imperfect people like me who are conflicted and trying to figure out their true purpose can go and get the assistance needed to continue the pursuit. I thought church would be that safe place for me. I assumed that those in leadership were trained to help equip me with the resources necessary for me to become skilled in the things of God. I assumed the way in which I handled instructions would be the proven record disclosing that I could be trusted with godly assignments, eventually resulting in my being a great asset to my local church. But instead, during that period, I felt like I was being judged. I felt like I was often placed under a microscope that had very limited capabilities to dissect the authentic me.

Sadly, I soon found out that their pleasantries were all lip service. They indirectly rejected me before ever giving me a chance to mature in the things of God. I was discouraged by the toxic things that I saw happening in church to people who didn't measure up to leadership's expectations or standards. Those lessons taught me how to be extremely cautious about anything or anyone remotely connected to church, especially those in leadership. My thought process about those in authority became lopsided, so I used this situation to my advantage to keep moving in the opposite direction of purpose and my making any formal commitment to another local church. I even gave God an out clause, as if He needed one. But in true Lisa fashion I pre-determined that God was way too busy to deal with me and all my foolishness, so He could just cross me of the list of workers who could potentially do great things for the kingdom. Putting it mildly, I had not yet come into the full realization that it's not the church that destroys people. No; what devastates people are the actions of unhealthy individuals who come into the church refusing to recognize, confront or even seek out help for their dysfunctions. They bring the same drama into the house of the Lord, labeling it as something different and unheard of. You know the term we use: "God is still working on me"? Well, inquiring minds often wonder when you are going to let God start the process. It is tragic but true that I myself have been guilty of bringing this same worldly behavior and mindset to the church, with no probability of changing my behavior. Instead of applying God's principles and unconditional love, I continued doing me, as if that version of me was all that! We all know it wasn't, but I used that version of myself as an excuse to make all my failed possibilities appear sensible. That is, until life got ridiculously overwhelming.

As the weight of life forced me to rethink my priorities, I found myself traveling this route that was leading me towards God more frequently until I finally convinced myself that God is the only solution I should be seeking. Strangely enough, it took almost a decade for my eyesight to become clear. I had a difficult time letting go of those unfortunate experiences in which I found out that not everyone confessing to know God truly has a real relationship with Him. Their actions spoke volumes. This made me analyze the condition of my own limited relationship with God, as well as the consequential choices I made when life got complicated that seemed to creatively attach themselves to my setbacks. As I began to surrender my ego, my will, my goals and my ambitions to the will of God for my life, the internal war increased. I felt trapped. I was trying to determine whether God could or would use somebody like me to do extraordinary things. My self-worth and identity were in crisis mode. With their infectious characters, doubt and unbelief reared up to join in the catastrophe. This combination substantially tried to undermined my belief that God was not like some of the people I encountered in church.

There were those who saw something unique, special and unorthodox in me and, rather than help to cultivate that thing I had not yet made sense of, they chose to misuse and mishandle me. I figured out quickly that vulnerability placed in the wrong hands is dangerous. As it turns out my responses were upsetting protocol because they were not the norm. I was in the infancy stage of my walk with Christ, so I was clueless. I didn't know the questions I asked were difficult: questions about purpose for me and the church, about hearing the voice of God, God's principles for an abundant life, or how one determines and develops his or her gifts and talents. It shocked me that their answers were inadequate and provided no blueprint that I could follow. I wasn't looking for them to do the work for me; I just needed a place to start. I was seeking after truth and I assumed that the people confessing to know the word could at least point me in the right direction to find answers. Instead of loving, mentoring and nurturing me or my gifts and talents, it became more of a competition to see how quickly I would fail. They were allowing their ignorance to gain momentum and their immaturity to dictate their petty actions in order to try and terminate my contribution to the Kingdom. It's peculiar to see religious-minded people taking issue with the work of God being produced by the hands of the unexpected rather than by their own. Their ungodly actions proved that there is a huge difference between religion and relationship. It signified that they were more concerned with the promotion of tradition and self rather than the pathway to discipleship. I didn't know the power I possessed within called the Holy Spirit. I didn't know I was already pre-qualified. I didn't know that God had already endorsed me for the assignment and that approval by man was unnecessary. I didn't know that I was allergic to ordinary and that God was making excellence possible. I didn't know why God found it necessary to place something special inside of me that would produce a great harvest. However, I was certain that I was not what the folks in church expected, nor was I at all what they were looking for. It was evident by their inability to see me through the eyes of our Creator. They were more concerned with my outer appearance, while God was focused on my heart.

During this time, the foundation of my relationship with God was anything but stable. This made it more difficult than it had to be for me to fully grasp how to identify my real purpose. I let my focus slip into some areas of darkness and negativity that tried to persuade me that I was unfit for such a task. I was having episodes of psychological distress trying to figure out who I was. I kept defining myself by my deficiencies and reminding myself that I don't have what it takes to succeed in purpose. After all, I have no formal training in theology. To make matters worse, I listened to the voices of people who didn't understand my purpose and paid far too much attention to my feelings. Through those ins and outs, I disqualified myself. My inability to describe, argue, define, explain or persuade my purpose silenced my voice. I was stuck in a downward spiral trying to figure out how to get out. I grew tired of speculating as to the meaning of my purpose. Disappointment set in because I couldn't understand the righteousness of God placed down on the inside of me.

Ignorance is not an appropriate excuse to forfeit destiny; however, over time, trying to make sense of purpose started to drain me. The images of the lives I was supposed to affect made me nervous. In my eyes, I had wasted so much time already and still I was nowhere closer to being able to offer anything of substance about my purpose. I fought against the option to quit in solitude. The thought of my not being able to blossom in my purpose or, for that matter, to appreciate its worth was giving me anxiety. With caution, I tried to conjure up the confidence to move past the vow I had mindlessly made to not commit to a local church ever again. Something let me know that God was not playing with me and, if purpose was really what I was after, it was major decision time.

My problem was not with God; it was more about how God was going to develop my faith in Him to use me in any capacity. He was asking me to subject myself to the good and bad aspects of belonging to a local assembly in order to stretch my reliance for Him. He wanted me to stop being so self-centered and shift direction towards who God is to me. I felt anxious as I knew I would have do that which I had vowed I would never do. Humility at this point was not my best attribute; my pride had to be diminished for that to shine. I had to acknowledge the fact that my belonging to a local congregation would be taxing but profitable as well, a statement I wasn't completely ready to claim as my truth. I knew that my decision would push me out of my comfort zone, and that scenario scared me. The noise in my head started getting louder. I didn't want to rehash those painful moments or the heart-rending memories of my interactions with former church members. All these recollections were pushing me into choosing to opt-out before my purpose even had a chance to take off. Thankfully, God did not approve of this tactic.

As the distractions grew in intensity, my anxiety grew, and my thoughts turned again to questioning the character of those who professed to represent God. To plead my case, I repeatedly shared my struggles involving those in authority to God emphasizing how they freely admitted to hearing the voice of God, yet their actions proved otherwise. Adding to my list of suspicious characters, I included those meaningful strangers whose guidance, as profound as it was meant to be, fell on deaf ears. Unconsciously I would shake my head while uttering under my breath, "They don't have a clue." I can remember politely saying "Thank you" and quickly walking away from some of them, knowing this action was for their benefit, not mine. I just wanted to avoid appearing disinterested or rude. I was screaming internally as the memories kept flooding my thoughts. I simply wanted to forget all the church hurt I had ever experienced.

Lumping the church and its leadership into one nice tidy box that I never needed to re-open and address allowed me to stay stationary. I used the acts of those I once trusted as a creditable excuse to cave to my own self-centered will. How could this turn out so wrong? I was looking for a way out, but no reasonable way was available. I wanted to just disappear. I wanted to erase the memories from the relationships that only fostered my belief that God would not select a person with such a colorful background as mine to equip with great gifts and talents for a historic purpose. In tears, those images of my being controlled by the opinions of others and not God's infuriated and disappointed me. The unexpected, tactless, and unkind treatments I suffered under shaky questionable church leadership fostered insecurity, uncertainty, and apprehension in me, which I still regularly fight to immobilize. I wanted the uproar to stop all at once. I needed to hear from God himself. Only He had the power to calm my spirit, but I was having difficulty locating the throne room of God because my prayer life was what you would consider scarce.

My lack of a committed prayer life and unanticipated harsh treatment drove me directly into the arms of fear, panic and distrust. Trust me; nothing good ever derives from a place where you are afraid, in terror or suspicious, except an acceptance of a mediocre life surrounded by many invisible glass walls you consider protection.

The wounds from being mishandled by those in authority led me down the path of isolation, which I admittedly used as a diversion to dodge rejection. I permitted their actions to make me feel insignificant, and I released my control to the enemy, rather than to God. I used my unhealthy emotions to create barriers so as to avoid building true Christian friendships. This was not the case in my childhood, so I was agonizing about the difference. I was a young adult in my late twenties, naive and vibrant with a desire to make a difference for the Lord, when the attacks came without warning. Being near religious leaders in authority who were consumed by their own selfish desires quenched my quest to go after purpose. But on a brighter note it did increase my level of understanding of Romans 11:29 Amplified Bible (AMP), "For the gifts and the calling of God are irrevocable [for He does not withdraw what He has given, nor does He change His mind about those to whom He gives His grace or to whom He sends His call]." The fact that they were unable to see the pain they inflicted was sickening. I had the wrong idea in believing I could be the recipient they would positively cultivate. It is such a shame that they overlook the opportunity to be a blessing to a person who is not in position to further their own personal agendas, giving little or no consideration to the vows they made to God in public settings.

I became more discouraged every time I rehashed those moments, and my respect for those in authority in the church declined. It is not uncommon to observe leaders without integrity in the world, but to see this same type of behavior in church threw me for one serious curveball. I was disgusted by the ways in which I was neglected. I was shocked by the full-scale operations they undertook to shatter the utilization of my God-given gifts and talents that were meant for the advancement of God's Kingdom. I struggled with making sense of why God would set me up in places with people who were resistant to helping me navigate my way to accomplishing purpose. My mind kept drifting in ethical directions trying to figure how someone in authority can choose to opt out of aiding those in need. Because their practices were not reasonably logical or intelligible, I did what most of us do; I consciously second-guessed my decision to return to church. My indecisiveness didn't mean that I didn't believe in God or that I would not ever attend church services; no, my decision simply affirmed that committing entirely to any aspect of a local church was not a good idea. Sadly, this decision only indicated that I put more faith in the power of man than I did in God or His promises for me. I didn't understand at the time that God was teaching me how to completely trust and depend on Him. I didn't understand that this was the avenue that would reveal to me how to recognize God as a provider, healer, a way maker, a comforter, and as a friend who sticks closer than a brother to me.

Despite these hurdles, my relationship with God was constantly changing. It was progressing from our being acquaintances to a more official status, but not quite BFFs. I found myself in an unusual place, desiring to be in His presence more and more. I was fascinated by and attentive to God, but I wanted no part of church. As insane as that sounds, that worked for me for a while. The repercussion of my choices didn't matter; I was willing to test my fate. I was clueless as to the impact my actions would have on fulfilling my purpose. I was deceiving myself believing that lessening the pursuit to totally commit to God and the things of God wasn't so bad. However, the disarray from this decision would become apparent as time went on. I had one foot in my comfort zone - i.e. the world - and one foot with Jesus, and we all know that never works long-term. At some point you will discover you cannot effectively love two masters. You will love one and hate the other or vice versa, until a voluntary choice is made.

Thinking back, very little deep consideration was given to the consequences of my actions, although I always seemed be in some sort of strenuous debate with God about His capability of delivering on what He promised. The untimeliness of the periodic comparisons of my dreams with the exchanges shared by strangers had me in shambles. In my attempts to deny purpose I was essentially placing more emphasis on my own personal life goals without any consideration of whether they agreed with the plan of God for my life. That made all my teachable moments, which were meant to shape my values and my priorities, a waste. I was signing my life away, because a life not anchored in God will ultimately lead you down the path of destruction. You know the saying: God takes care of babes and fools, well I easily fell into both categories. I was being dangerously defiant by resisting purpose. Frustrating truth, the energy I exerted trying to reject the assignment appeared at the time a much easier concept to grasp than believing God. It was not obvious to me that my focus was being redirected by the church struggles I experienced and that I was generously relinquishing the power that could potentially jeopardize my future. Seeing the abstract vision that exceeded my expectations added to the unsolicited pressure making the situation worse. Its greatness was overwhelming, especially through my misconception of self, so I just contested.

Still, purpose continued in hot pursuit, making me a target for the most crucial work I would ever undertake. God was requiring me to extend unconditional love to all humanity. He wanted me to give of myself unselfishly to those whose hearts had been damaged just like mine, and I never saw it coming. Fortunately, I learned how to labor in the throne room of God's grace; not an expeditious process, I might add. My negotiations with God to delegate someone more qualified and skilled than me became useless. I tried to play up the idea that I am no expert in unconditional love, as if God was unaware of my capabilities. My only undisputed reference of true sacrificial love was my sons. Still, God refused to subscribe to my channel.

It was during this season of my life that I became open to the incredible possibilities of my assignment and its potential risks. The venue didn't matter. It could be at the nail shop, the grocery store, the gas station, or at the movies; God is not prejudiced. People settling for pint-sized love when they deserved gallon-sized love would somehow be near to me. Exchanges like these are very challenging, especially if they are not orchestrated by God. You must be confident that God Himself called and chose you as an intercessor - a person who intervenes on behalf of others through prayer - because their emotions are felt as if they are your own. Without the approval of God, you will burn out easily, cave under pressure, and do more damage than good because of impure motives.

As I think of all the people who have crossed my path, it is evident why the lessons I intensely scrutinized and tried to avoid at all cost were necessities. Resisting and denying purpose is no longer a plausible outcome for me. Each experience I encounter reminds me of the underserved unconditional love that Jesus offered to me: a love I know I could never earn or deserve. Thankfully, the deposit of this great love is not pointless. On any given day, I am drawn to people who have lost their hope and their situations appear bleak. God challenges me to offer authentic love in many of those discouraging circumstances. These situations tugged and pulled at my heart stings until I discharged a giant-sized gift of unconditional love that at times is not eagerly received. The deeds I once considered small and the surmounted hardships endured are all platforms being used by God to keep me pursuing purpose in a culture that believes this type of love is extinct.

The revolving door of my guarded heart where comfort and ordinariness reign has lost its appeal. In this era, despite my short comings, I am certain that every event leading up to this point and beyond will continue to thrust me into the pre-arranged plan God designed for my life. I had no clue that being unapologetically different would be an asset for my faith walk to thrive. I had no clue that at the least opportune times I would be placed in predicaments in which my character, attitude and the level of faith I projected would be used to confound the wise. I had no clue that my gifts and talents would provide opportunities, or that my true character and integrity would sustain and safeguard my purpose. I had no clue that in countless ways my faith would have to endure violent outbreaks as purpose was executed. It took my exposure to James 1:2-12 Amplified Bible (AMP):

> Consider it nothing but joy, my [a]brothers and sisters, whenever you fall into various trials. Be assured that the testing of your faith [through experience] produces endurance [leading to spiritual maturity, and inner peace]. And let endurance have its perfect result and do a thorough work, so that you may be perfect and completely developed [in your faith], lacking in nothing. If any of you lacks wisdom [to guide Him through a decision or circumstance], He is to ask of [our benevolent] God, who gives to everyone generously and without rebuke or blame, and it will be given to him. But He must ask [for wisdom] in faith, without doubting [God's willingness to help], for the one who doubts is like a billowing surge of the sea that is blown about and tossed by the wind. For such a person ought not to think or expect that He will receive anything [at all] from the Lord, being a double-minded man, unstable and restless in all His ways [in everything He thinks, feels, or decides]. Let the brother in humble circumstances glory in His high position [as a born-again believer, called to the true riches and to be an heir of God]; and the rich man is to glory in being humbled [by trials

revealing human frailty, knowing true riches are found in the grace of God], for like the flower of the grass He will pass away. For the sun rises with a scorching wind and withers the grass; its flower falls off and its beauty fades away; so too will the rich man, during His pursuits, fade away. Blessed [happy, spiritually prosperous, favored by God] is the man who is steadfast under trial and perseveres when tempted; for when He has passed the test and been approved, He will receive the [victor's] crown of life which the Lord has promised to those who love Him."

These words concerning God, His love, wisdom, faith and purpose affirmed how misguided my views were. I didn't anticipate reaching purpose in the same manner in which I handle trials and tribulations. I had convinced myself that the pathway to purpose doesn't require all of that. Yet in the same breath, I was questioning why the many blessings I desired had not yet manifested. I had failed to see that persecution was the scaffolding used for me to accept purpose; that is, until God quietly whispered the enchanting and amazing words found in Ephesians 3:18-21 Amplified Bible (AMP);

Be fully capable of comprehending with all the saints (God's people) the width and length and height and depth of His love [fully experiencing that amazing, endless love]; and [that you may come] to know [practically, through personal experience] the love of Christ which far surpasses

[mere] knowledge [without experience], that you
may be filled up [throughout your being] to all
the fullness of God [so that you may have the
richest experience of God's presence in your lives,
completely filled and flooded with God Himself].
Now to Him who is able to [carry out His purpose
and] do superabundantly more than all that we
dare ask or think [infinitely beyond our greatest
prayers, hopes, or dreams], according to His
power that is at work within us, to Him be the
glory in the church and in Christ Jesus throughout
all generations forever and ever. Amen.

The core of my soul vibrated as God's love penetrated every
ounce of my being. I had to tell myself that the opinions of
others whether they know me or not, have no power to define
how I see myself unless I let them. Whenever life gets foggy the
words in this chapter assure me that the mask I once used as
protection will no longer provide the security I once believed it
did. It did not matter that I was not what they expected, nor is
my value predicated on their perception. I was pre-determined
by God Himself.

As I am maturing in the things of God, I am confident that
God can now trust me with His love purpose because we have
history. I want His love to be visible by the way in which I
love others. With my renewed mind and pure heart, I had the
courage to put an end to the messiness of life that regularly
tried to distract me. The attacks of those who viciously fought
against me were fruitless in their endeavors. As the Word says,
"He will make your enemies your footstools." My failure to

see myself as God sees me ceased to be a deterrent, because I now share the same vision of myself as He does. The power of influence I possess through His holy spirit cannot be denied, as is the threat to silence my purpose. Being led by the holy spirit has its perks, I now anticipate the enemy's attempts to use those closest to me to divert my efforts with intensity, so I am prepared. Ephesians 6:12 Amplified Bible (AMP), tells me:

> For our struggle is not against flesh and blood [contending only with physical opponents], but against the rulers, against the powers, against the world forces of this [present] darkness, against the spiritual forces of wickedness in the heavenly (supernatural) places. I now have a pattern to follow that will fulfill God's plan. My entire life thus far has been the preparation needed for my purpose to be discovered. I am learning how to resist the urge to hide or downgrade my gifts and talents, while faithfully encouraging others regardless if I am appreciated or not. It has already been established that my rewards do not come from people. I refuse to reduce my devotion of God simply because of their illiteracy. I am secure in who I am, noting that future generations are counting on my flourishing. By my putting my past where it belongs, in the past, by letting God reign in His rightful place, by walking daily in purpose, I win.

As I continued my grind, I truly came to terms with my purpose process and how it was exactly what I needed for humility to arise. It is the one characteristic that is essential in revealing my dependency on God. My unstable emotions and distressing memories were no longer regulating my heart. The attempts to regurgitate my past, with its potential to disqualify me for greatness, subsided. The unsolicited attacks that were to undermine my creditability were used as a platform for my purpose. God in His heavenly wisdom ushered me from a person with a survival mentality to one with a momentous purpose. My worth mounted, and my value increased as His love overflows. I had to own my decision to run counterclockwise to purpose, hoping never to be caught.

When I established responsibility for the faulty condition of our relationship, the obstruction blocking my flow to God began to vanish. I could feel God stabilizing me through the tears that fell from my eyes. I am thankful to God for providing both and, although I did not pray for purpose or a place of worship, both were integral to my development. A quick reflection of the people who pretended to be holy to convince immature believers like myself that we must reflect their characteristics to be known as a representative of God brings tears to my eyes, and I wonder how many had to travel that road to learn that difficult lesson. How many had to discover that what was offered as safe and secure was an imposter? The pain from it all was still very vivid and real for me. I used every attempt to blame in order to avoid and confront my own failures. I was seeking after real forgiveness, for the good, the not so good and everything in between. In prayer I freely admitted my need for and dependency on God. This powerful place of freedom is what invigorates me to continue my intimate prayer life. In those sessions controversies were resolved, while knowledge and understanding were gained. It unlocked my heart, mind and soul in such an unspeakable way. My purpose unfolded without interruption. For the first time in a long while, I could no longer deny the power of prayer. My heart didn't feel contaminated, and the transformation wasn't frightening like I envisioned. I desired what God wanted for my life.

More times than I can count, God continues to remind me of all we endured together so I will hold on to purpose with a tight grip. During those exchanges, He instructs me how to not complicate or overthink what He has already made achievable. When I begin to question the timing, wondering whether I could have discovered my purpose sooner, God gently reminds me of who is in control. He reminds me that we are in sync now or, as the mill lumens say, "our squad is tight." God's plan is doable and manageable because I understand the importance of obedience. God reminds me not to distract myself with things that don't concern me and to trust that He knows what He is doing. In other words, I need to stay in my own lane and be about my Father's business - the purpose of reliable love. He repeatedly reminds me that the love purpose is a never-ending calling that is achieved by those who endure. Without questioning, I yield to His command. I am on God's timetable, so I am not alone in this thing. I forge ahead, aware that the miscellaneous disturbances are indicators that growth and expansion are accessible. I am confident that my required faith and works to rise above are available. So, risking all to achieve destiny is intentional for me, because I understand that I am being fueled by His strength. I am firmly aware of my sphere of influence and realize that what I do or not do will affect generations yet to come. Despite the uncertainty in life, I find comfort in what I know to be true that only love can force out purpose - and I have barely scratched the surface. Wait and watch; the love purpose will prevail.

chapter 4

Family

One Tuesday morning my family experienced a terrible calamity. When I picked up the phone, I thought that the words coming through the receiver had to be wrong. Some part of me knew it couldn't be a lie, since it was my sister's voice delivering the message, but I was unsure. As I shut my eyes, the words kept echoing inside my head: "Dino is dead"; "Dino is dead". Screaming and trembling were the only two behavioral responses I could conjure up in that moment. I became paralyzed by my own personal thoughts. I was struggling, trying to connect the dots. According to natural law, parents are supposed to leave the earth before their children. My parents were still alive, so how could this be?

I was devastated and in shock. My brother Dino was dead, and nothing that I had ever experienced in my life thus far could have prepared me for his unexpected death. He wasn't sick and he hadn't been in a car accident. No; some deranged individual deliberately decided that his life was pointless and ended it on that day. My big brother was gone, and I never imagined having to live in this world without him. Flashes of his wife and two infant sons invaded my thoughts. His sons would never know him or have a relationship with him now. The more I replayed those thoughts, the angrier I became. The fact that he would never see his sons graduate from elementary school, high school or even college, for that matter, intensified my rage. Someone had stolen all the wonderful opportunities he should have had to see his sons go on their first dates, get married and have children of their own. The array of emotions was consuming me as I tried to suppress them. I could see myself drifting to a dark place where no light existed. Struggling not to feel, I moved from denial to wanting to be isolated, to bargaining with God and, eventually, acceptance.

This death experience got my attention in more ways than one. It reminded me of all the times I was fixated on begging God not to allow anything awful to happen to me while my children were young. The possibility of my being murdered was not on my radar at all. But thoughts of my life ending abruptly and early, before my children grew to adulthood, were at the forefront of my mind now. My requests were not selfishly motivated. You see, from my early childhood my health has always been under attack. For most of my life I have suffered from chronic pain, female disorders, migraines, bronchitis, allergies and asthma, just to name a few of my ailments. I agonized over what could potentially happen to my sons if I died prematurely. My brother's death reminded me of how I pleaded with God to let me live until my youngest son was at least eighteen years old. Even though it would have been difficult for them to endure, I was raising them to depend on each other, which would give them the resilience to go on. I thought about my plan in detail. I prayed that, if it were to happen, my youngest son would be at least eighteen. This would ensure that they both would be legal adults and there was far less likelihood of them being separated. I have seen first-hand how some family members and friends make elaborate plans for what they would do in cases of emergencies, even going as far as to vow to take full responsibility for the minor child or children if the parent or parents were incapable of performing their parental duties or succumbed to an untimely death. Although their intentions were good, I have also lived long enough to see some of those same family members and friends disappear and/or have selective amnesia about the commitments they declared while the person was in need or alive. This was the dark cloud I had to deal with in my own family, which had the potential to threaten the heritage of future generations.

My family dynamics are far from ideal. Like most families, we have our own fair share of dysfunction. My parents are both Bahamian, so island culture is our foundation. However, my father spent most of his life stateside or, as we say back home, he's American now. My first recollection of living in a two-parent household wasn't until my mother decided we were moving to join my father in Glasgow, Scotland, where my father was gainfully employed. Prior to that announcement, I have no recollection of my parents living under the same roof. I did hear stories about it, but nothing from my own memory. I'm sure there were reasons for the separation periods, but that is their story to tell, not mine. Plus, the Word promises me that when I honor my mother and father, long life is my reward, and I desire a long life.

Now, moving to Scotland sounds exciting. We traveled across international waters and we even lived in a castle. But as a nine-year-old little girl who had lived most of her life in the Bahamas surrounded by family and friends, this was traumatic, and it wasn't just because of the difference in the weather. In the Bahamas, our living arrangements were often communal. My mom, my siblings and I lived with our maternal grandmother and my two uncles for most of my childhood years. This was my initial foundation of family life; that is, until my mother decided she wanted to spread her wings and express her independence. So, for me, the family structure is dramatically diverse. It shifted from Grandma's house to my independent Mom's house and then to a two-parent household in a foreign country. I'm sure these patterns were not totally in sync with God's design for raising a family, but it is what it is. In some way they all aided in forming the woman that I am now. Entering my early adult life, I occasionally wondered who I would have become if our family structure was configured totally according to the blueprint of God. However, I stopped myself from exhausting unnecessary energy on it, because I do know that history cannot be re-written, no matter how much we ponder it. Instead, I spent time questioning whether some of the family issues we encountered - those we survived with detectable scars as well as the unsolved ones that we continue to pretend don't exist for the sake of fabricated peace - would life be different.

In observing the family into which I was born, I realize just how extremely rare God's sense of humor is. We all have these unstated and preconceived ideas of what the family unit should resemble. Our perception of each other is somewhat swayed by biological, social, and personal experiences and biases. As interesting as perception can be, when its purpose is self-gratification, it can be quite disruptive. We predetermine who we deem to be the favorite by how someone is treated by those responsible and contributing to our well-being, never considering that the additional preference given may simply mean that individual requires extra to thrive at life. There are countless, unspoken family roles assigned without consent solely based on opinions. Key misleading assumptions, the unrealistic expectations we have for each other merely because we are biologically linked, the way we respond within the family when unexpressed expectations go unfilled or how we respond when misunderstandings that threaten to tear us all apart are heightened. However, the leading misconception that is often privately discussed at intimate gatherings is who the black sheep of the family is. For those who don't know its meaning, "**black sheep**" is an idiom used to describe an odd or disreputable member of a **family**. We seem to forget that we are all guilty of making mistakes that we are not thrilled about or care to repeat. With that fact in mind, every one of us at one time or another feels like they are the black sheep of the family; especially when our failures are repeatedly mentioned at family get-togethers as if they are one big joke - as if we have the power to rewrite our errors. Surely, everyone must know by now that if we could have omitted those questionable actions from our journey or, at a minimum, recreated our past, we would gladly have exercised that option.

We make assumptions about each other's abilities, character traits, significant others, financial obligations, money management skills and value. Of course, these assumptions are rarely ever vocalized to the family member being secretly discussed. What exactly is the motive behind our actions? We assume that everyone in our family owns their own special crystal ball that gives voice to all our unexpressed emotions, hidden desires and unspoken needs, requiring no action on our part to personally participate in a real, eye-opening, true-life conversation to put the matters to rest. However, if criticism were to arise, typically under distress, we release unhealthy, unreasonable and unproductive responses to the conflict, allowing the retaliation to escalate to where we become defensive saying something along the lines of "You should know what I am dealing with or going through," or "You should be aware of how I feel about such and such," followed up by the guilt move, "After all, we are family and isn't family supposed to be there for each other?" How absurd is this logic? How can I possibly be guilty of not caring about someone else's mental anguish if they haven't chosen to divulge all the information to me? How heartbreaking is it to find yourself positioned in the seat of judgement for a crime you didn't even know you committed?

As time elapses and situations and circumstances don't change, we cling to the unhealthy habit of remaining on the damaging pathway, dying inside due to pride, which keeps us from apologizing. You know we will wear that pride badge of honor like a decorated soldier. We don't even seem to realize that it only supports our downward spiral into seclusion, as depression throws a bulls-eye for the mind. To play it safe - or at least that's our perception - we enter a self-protective mode, using disconnection and withdrawal practices as a way to avoid fully investing in beneficial resolutions to resolve conflict. Through the years, I have been guilty of demonstrating these exact qualities without ever giving a hint of understanding to the stance of the family member I deem to love. Because of my dislike of uncertainty, I would opt out of giving effort to cultivating committed family relations in hopes of avoiding sensibly negotiating compromising terms that would benefit all parties involved. Instead, I focused more on preventing myself from being vulnerable, hurt, embarrassed, exploited or misunderstood. I used petty, immature excuses to hide behind as justification, repeatedly letting unresolved issues keep me separated from what I desired the most - a loving connection with my family. Instead of giving intentional effort to stop or prevent division, I smoke screened my real fears and funneled my energy into being more tolerant of similar offenses made by others. I'm sure those I love were confused as to whether I was really offended by some particular action.

One would think this exercise was pointless, but it was here I was able to face the truth about how I handled family discord. It also sparked my curiosity to learn how to better handle these kinds of stumbling blocks. Great news: at this stage of the game, I was smart enough to know that if I wanted lasting solutions, I needed my instructions to come from the Creator of family, not from the advice columns found on the web. I thought it would be quite helpful to find out why the Creator established family in the first place, and not just the part about being fruitful and multiplying. I wanted to understand God's deliberate intentions for family. How are we to fill and subdue the earth and be the essential building block of human society? If this knowledge would make my family better, I was all in. I looked-for answers, because my family deserved better; in fact, *I* deserved better. I wanted us to have deeper, more meaningful relationships, so I had to address the issues that promoted chaos.

With numerous thought-provoking questions, I started my dialogue with God who, by the way, is very transparent when you make yourself available. It is impressive and frightening all at the same time. My exchange of questions went from zero to one hundred with God. I was convinced that my introductory question was profound: "Why is family so important to you, God?" Profound or not, it uncovered some interesting facts. From its existence, family is intended to be the first environment where we learn about God and how to live for Him. Parents are meant to influence their children towards Christ through teaching and the example they set in the home. If, in the home environment, physical, emotional, social, economic and spiritual lessons are practiced daily, the family will be enabled to become productive citizens. This explanation seems simple, until you must put it into motion. I was hungry; my appetite for understanding was craving more, so I continued to dig deeper to find out what all this entails. A little sweat was not going to deter me from discovering practical solutions that I could implement into my everyday life to ensure productive development for my family.

However, I wasn't prepared for what God was requiring of me personally. To accomplish the will of God I had to be willing to let go of all my unhealthy behavior, which I used as excuses to avoid truth. If I chose the path of least resistance, like numerous families who lack interest for the things of God, the effects of family breakdown can be as destructive as the effects of injustice. Just look at today's trends; they already forecast a significant collapse in the stability of the family unit if major changes are not implemented. Until we hit the reset button, the Church - by default - will have to continue being the source to introduce the family to God, along with continuing with its primary function of providing training and opportunities that join people of all nations together with different gifts to preserve God's work for future generations. Ironically, a similar disorder is plaguing our educational system. If we look behind the walls of many of the schools throughout the country, we see that while teachers were initially hired to educate our children, as time has elapsed, the influence of society has caused a tremendous increase in their workload. In addition to educating students, teachers have been forced into the position of assuming a number of parental responsibilities, as well. As a result, we are living in a confused culture due to our failure to preserve the important tradition of rearing children in the ways of the Lord. We have stopped modelling the life He called us to live and opted for reality tv as our guidance. We forgot that how we live and who we are makes a difference, overlooking the fact that family is God's greatest expression of love to mankind.

This insight challenged me to question why the traditional family has gotten so far off track and is so often under attack. At first glance it appears that God's love for family is what drives the assault; however, as true as that remark is, it is only a portion of the equation. As I investigated a little further, I discovered that the enemy persistently strives to use his power to confuse our views about who we are in Christ, as well as to confuse us about the purpose and benefits of godly families. Sadly, in today's climate, Christians find it far more difficult to reject the constantly corroding culture we face than to cling to biblical truth, as if what we are experiencing in culture is such a blessing. We are forgetting that Satan's ultimate purpose is to destroy the Christian family. He is famous for manipulating us so that we doubt anything remotely connected to God. By working towards that goal with increased intensity, frequency and cleverness, we have allowed the attacks to complicate our understanding of God and His promises for us. The opposition is so crafty that he works diligently to make sure we see our lives as miserable so that we discredit God. But I must remind you that regardless of what Satan - or today's culture - attempts to do to minimize the importance of a godly family, the family will always be the principal building block of humanity. With the impelling of the Holy Spirit we must fight to ensure our righteous nature is not polluted by worldly culture, by remaining steadfast and doing our part to protect and defend its value. We cannot afford to let the enemy erase God's righteousness from influencing the world of His design for family for future generations. We must boldly let our lights shine in such a powerful way that the world will take notice. This task will not be easy, but robust resilience is key to achieving greatness. When we fully commit ourselves to a lifestyle of righteousness, obedience, forgiveness and compassion, we will begin to comprehend why God delegated authority to mankind. We are accountable for what happens on earth. We must execute an intentional prayer life that includes medication of scriptures and our embracing wisdom, even when we are dismayed. We must spearhead the fight against godly families and bring awareness of its benefits. When we aim our efforts to continuously and correctly use the gifts and talents that have been entrusted to us, we win.

To reclaim my family for the Kingdom, I needed a well-defined, vivid vision that would foster the values of God. My first action item was to examine my own attributes to see what adjustments I needed to make to regain stability in correlation with God's blueprint. With the help of the Holy Spirit I am continuously making modifications. Once a significant number of layers of misinformation were replaced with godly knowledge, I was able to understand that to truly regain my family, I had to be willing to be the first partaker of change. I rolled the decision to be the first over and over until I finally submitted. It felt unachievable at first, but I discovered in situations that appear bleak, God does the impossible. I just had to be willing to start first, which, while difficult, would allow me to maintain some form of control. As the saying goes, pray until something happens, well that something started happening within me. As God cleansed my heart, renewed my mind and opened my eyes to how broken I was, I became able to see how some of my prior efforts and actions had been more of a deterrent than a blessing to my family. The process was teaching me how to resist the need to be reckless with the life God has granted me. He pruned me to fulfill my godly appointed role in the family. As a result, I changed my presentation but not my mission. I still desired every member of my family to be saved and to live a righteous prosperous life, but not at the expense of my badgering them with scriptures. I didn't want to be contentious or combative. I wanted what God wanted; a family built on the foundation of love - the defining characteristic of a spiritual family. I found comfort in knowing that as I nurtured, protected and loved my family, all those attributes would someday become contagious and be returned to me. God dared me to believe that family love is forever present. With the seemingly small things I did from my heart, God continues to produce amazing results.

chapter 5

Friends

What I have unraveled over the years as my truth is that a true friend has a comparable role in my life to that of a healthy biological family member. Even though we have been given the authority of selecting our friends while our biological families are chosen for us, they both share common interests in our life journey. These relationships play a dominant role in our destiny progression. They should both inspire us to be the best version of ourselves and aid us to flourish at this thing called life. They should encourage us in our quest to define who we are as individuals as we continuously work at developing our characters. I would like to say that as far back as I can recall, my circle of friends was founded on these powerful defining principles. However, that would be untrue - mainly due to my innocence and my vague understanding of the concept of friendships at the time. I was probably somewhere between the ages of four and five years old when my initial exposure to people I labeled as friends manifested. This most likely occurred at a local playground, or perhaps in a classroom or at the home of a friend of my mother, where I am certain I couldn't yet articulate the traits that would qualify someone as a true friend. Nor for that matter could I recognize the attributes in the individuals I claimed as my friends. It's funny how in our youth we can so easily attach the word "friend" to someone we know very little about simply because they played nice with us at the park and shared their toys. I laugh out loud thinking how life would be a breeze if this was the only essential quality needed for a person to be considered a true friend. If only life could have stayed in such a simple, unpretentious state; regrettably, however, I found out it doesn't.

As we grow into adulthood, we awkwardly enter the complex world of friendship in a lopsided manner, with minimal experiences to appropriately guide us in our attempts to decipher who is a genuine friend and who is merely an associate. In today's culture, especially, we see how far too many adults consider the number of followers that like their comments or pictures on social media as legitimate friends.

In the infancy stage of adulthood (if you remember your twenties, you'll understand, if not, you'll soon find out) you are more inclined to be slightly naïve as to the difference between acquaintances, casual associates and authentic friendships. The significant difference can be quite conflicting, especially when your self-worth is damaged and in danger. Regretfully, when your vision is impaired, and you primarily focus on your faults, your flaws and your failures, you fail to cautiously pay attention to your circle of influence, and you miss the evaluation process that helps to decode the differences. We ignore the undeniable signs of superficial friendships, even when the evidence undoubtingly reflects their lack of commitment towards us. And if that's not bad enough, we dismiss the fact that they are not fully invested in the alliance. We turn a blind eye to their issues while being embarrassed by our own actions. The amount of quality time we willingly invest in people who want to be obligation-free when it comes to a relationship with us is bizarre. We put ourselves through all sorts of turmoil trying to justify friendships that yield no positive results, simply to avoid appearing reckless and incapable of determining the creditability of that person close to our heart. We constantly make lame excuses for their conduct because, from our perspective, that direction appears to be far easier for us to digest than the alternative. The harsh reality of removing a person you deeply care for from your innermost circle because of their resistance to be authentic in the relationship is petrifying. So, to escape from our terrorizing thoughts, we predetermine the effort is far too risky, and we settle back into our comfort zone, resisting the urge to sensibly confront the subject. We have masterminded how to ignore the red flags, even though everyone else who is privy to our intimate space can hear the alarm bells ringing from miles away. We tend to place more effort into camouflaging our true feelings in hopes of preventing feelings of isolation and loneliness. Few of us are truly willing to make such a sacrifice to assess the value of a friendship. With the commodity of honesty being so diluted in our culture, we refrain from sharing our true feelings because it takes courage and provides an opening for opposition to silence our voices. We have become skeptical of people in general. Therefore, it is more difficult for us to fully believe and trust that authentic friendships are possible and achievable especially when it comes to friends who love unconditionally, give wise counsel, remain loyal, forgive easily, and promote our well-being unselfishly.

The images of this type of friendship hits home for me. I found myself having to stop and survey my own personal friendships. This exploit required me to be still as I examined each relationship independently. I discreetly and attentively mediated as I waited for God to reveal whether those close to my heart were truly my authentic friends or simply enthusiastic fans. Initially, the driving force that provoked my decision to tackle this assignment was a casual statement by a friend. She had no idea how her words, "all of your friends are very different", impacted my assessment. Her statement divulged that, from her observation, none of my friends showed any obvious similarities. Yet to me, they all had something very much in common. They were all critical individuals with the ability to influence my propelling towards or away from destiny. They each provided something distinctly different that was - and still is - to some degree needed for me to continue forging ahead on the pathway God envisioned for my life. Yet it was not crystal clear to me what those attributes were and how they would benefit the friendship while bringing glory to the Kingdom. It takes real life, demanding circumstances to truly know if those you consider friends are linked to your destiny. When life happens, and it will, people lose loved ones, both unexpectedly and expectedly, every day. Divorce, sickness, a new marriage, raising children, taking care of aging parents, career changes, money issues, and ministry are all examples of real-life circumstances that will test the foundation of any friendship. I had to mature quite a bit too fully grasp the entire meaning of the required investment for a true friendship to endure. I had to accept without doubting that if my true friendships were to survive the test of time, there were things

I would have to be prepared to execute, if necessary. Crying wolf should not exist in these relationships. First, I had to stay committed to the fact that true friendships do exist, and that they are attainable for me. This is problematic in today's culture; since most people we meet hide behind so many walls, it takes the patience of Job to break through the barriers to find the authentic person, particularly since they may still be in the process of trying to figure out ways to properly evict their representative. I had to foresee that throughout the journey both parties would hit curve balls that would test the footing of the relationship. During these times, each of us must be willing to remain steadfast and forward-thinking as we iron out our differences. I had to learn how to re-train my thought process to include the opinions of others as we maneuvered through our good and indifferent life experiences. There were and still will be moments when we will have to simply agree to disagree on certain topics if we truly desire to maintain our friendship. When necessary, together we must be willing to seek out ways to intercept the aftermath of those highly emotional conversations that can potentially hinder the lifelong friendships. Healthy, unhealthy or unmoved, the residue of those experiences will influence if or how we choose to pursue friendships with purpose. Until you have endured some of these casualties you are incapable of truly knowing if someone is indeed an authentic friend.

Since my level of understanding in this area was being enlightened, I found myself wanting to know more about God's definition of friendship. I wanted to know His intent as to why we even needed to engage or give energy to these types of relationships. As I examined the biblical description, a few qualities stood out compared to what defined my initial ideas of friendship. Godly friendships recognize that the friendship may be just for a season - until God's reason for the friendship is fulfilled, whereas, worldly friendships are all about the "self" and are bonded by the common interests and experiences we share. A great book that is filled with such intriguing knowledge about friendship is the book of Proverbs. I love the amplified version, but there are many translations out there, so do what works for you. Proverbs 17:17 Amplified Bible (AMP) explained how a friend loves at all times, and a brother is born for adversity; Proverbs 27:6 Amplified Bible (AMP): "Faithful are the wounds of a friend [who corrects out of love and concern], but the kisses of an enemy are deceitful" [because they serve His hidden agenda]; Proverbs 18:24 Amplified Bible (AMP): "The man of too many friends [chosen indiscriminately] will be broken in pieces and come to ruin, but there is a [true, loving] friend who [is reliable and] sticks closer than a brother"; Proverbs 27:17 Amplified Bible (AMP): "As iron sharpens iron, so one man sharpens [and influences] another" [through discussion]; Proverbs 13:20 Amplified Bible (AMP): "He who walks [as a companion] with wise men will be wise, but the companions of [conceited, dull-witted] fools [are fools themselves and] will experience harm". All these scriptures show us what to look for in true friendships. Once we are willing to provoke each another to demonstrate these qualities, our healthy life-long friendships will thrive.

Because of my yearning to understand more about real friendships, no one had to persuade me to continue the hunt. By studying, I stumbled across one of the most iconic friendships in the bible - the friendship between David and Jonathan.

We have all heard the story of David, the ruddy, bright-eyed shepherd boy who killed the giant Goliath, and some of us may be knowledgeable about the story of Jonathan, the son of Saul and the next heir to the throne whose life ended in his early forties during a battle with the Philistines. Unlike his father Saul, who was deficient in love, loyalty and faith, Jonathan was known for his deep love, loyal friendship, and faith in God. As I read the book of 1st Samuel, I learned how these two individuals formed an uncommon bond. They shared common interests and could have easily allowed their differences to destroy their bond but instead, those differences made it stronger. Their friendship sheds light on what a covenant relationship is. It is based upon a friendship that radiates mutual love and respect for each other, despite being from completely different backgrounds. Jonathan was a man born into privileged circumstances, while David was a man of modest means. Yet, through all their trials and tribulations, not once did they go against each other, and that is something we can all admire. Can you imagine the amount of discipline and trust in God it took for each one of them to remain fully committed when family and obstacles tried to separate them?

Inspired by their relationship, I investigated a little deeper into the friendship of David and Jonathan. There is no doubt that they understood how to grow separately without growing apart. Both men exhibited at least three unique qualities that are visible in godly friendships with purpose. True and upright friends will sacrifice for each other without hesitation. Secondly, true and upright friends are loyal to each other. Thirdly, true and upright friends can freely express their genuine emotions with one another without judgement. Their friendship is bonded by each other's love for God and obedience to His word and their individual callings. These same qualities should be visible in our friendship with Jesus. Check out John 15:13-15 Amplified Bible (AMP), which tells us that no one shows greater love [nor stronger commitment] than by laying down his own life for his friends. "You are my friends if you keep on doing what I command you. I do not call you servants any longer, for the servant does not know what his master is doing; but I have called you [My] friends, because I have revealed to you everything that I have heard from My Father." I want to defy the odds and see my friendship with Christ resemble that of Jonathan and David. Until I maintain this level of a lasting true friendship with Jesus, those friendships that I perceive as godly will start having the same characteristics as a worldly friendship. In the end, they will be short-lived and exhausting.

Thankfully, I am abundantly blessed in the friendship department. Through my life struggles, the faces of my circle of friends are meaningful, compassionate, and strong; they are a part of my reality, not just my memories. In many ways, they have demonstrated to me many of the powerful qualities visible in Jonathan and David's friendship. Their continuous efforts of support as God pours more into me for my journey is uncommon and sometimes underserved. Like I said before, my friends are the family I choose, and I pray I have chosen wisely. Has it been easy? No! It's not a far cry for me to shut down from everything and everyone, including my friends, because being vulnerable makes me feel helpless. At times, when fear and doubt crept in, urging me to choose the road of least resistance, I needed little convincing. But fortunately for me and those I love, I am learning how to resist the urge to let this condition intimidate the fight in me. I am learning how to be more resilient when unhealthy learned behavior that only produces habits that lack positive returns shows up, trying to take over. I recognize destructive emotional conduct as a red flag that can keep me from trusting in my noteworthy friendships, and so it requires an alternative response. I am learning to serve fear its eviction notice as I embrace a more productive habit, aligning my faith with the One that holds all the power to keep me from falling.

My dedication to each of my friends compels me to be careful about protecting the friendships I value. I am surrounded by their unconditional love, even when my actions don't always warrant that type of love response, especially during the tough times when I feel inadequate. They pray for me when I am unable to pray for myself. When I am sick, they have offered unwavering assistance without making me feel like a burden. They have provided wisdom and guidance in areas where my knowledge was not proficient and without making me feel foolish. They have used their fondness for me to turn my sadness into joy on the days that it felt as if the rain would never cease. They have made me appreciate the power of a hug and to be grateful for the silent conversations that only we understand. They have truly given new meaning to God's word that declares that two are better than one, because they have a good return for their labor. What started out as two people with similar casual interests grew into a friendship with someone who sees me, sees who I am, values and validates me. I am soaking up every one of God's principles for friendship so that my personal **growth will forever be enhanced.**

It has taken years for the meaning of authentic friendships to be fully comprehended by me. To stimulate continued growth, God continues to do routine pruning maintenance and I am discovering more facets in these relationships. The process of pruning is rarely easy, but it has freed my mind and spirit to adjust to the changes I am called to make. Once I incorporated the healthiness of authentic friendships into my life, God opened my heart to a dimension where my ability to love is out of this world. I stopped looking for ways to escape when circumstances created disagreements. I now use the guidance I acquired from God to find workable solutions. I started listening more to the heartbeat of the person I value for understanding instead of criticism. Even though I did the research backwards, those I consider to be real friends add so much value and joy to my life. I am so blessed to have the quality of friendships I have earned. I say "earned" because it costs me something to keep healthy relationships godly. They have front row seats to many chapters of my life and an awareness as to how I function. They are privy to my likes, dislikes, uncertainties, failures and successes and how I handle them, while affording me opportunities to grow pass my fears, insecurities and pain. My friends, who continue to bring out the best in me (and I in them) realize that there is always a greater level to grow when our priority is godly friendships that last a lifetime!

chapter 6

Money

Within the blink of an eye, I was over $150,000.00 in debt, and that did not include my mortgage or my car note. In my thirties that was a huge amount of debt, especially being a single parent with a less than moderate salary. I flash back to the many times I swiped the only working credit card in my wallet to purchase groceries for my children while praying that it would not be declined. It's mind-blowing to me how I survived some of the darkest financial times of my life. I admit I was no financial expert, but through experience I learned how to live on a budget. Of course, there were occasions when I may have splurged and added a little something extra to the shopping cart for myself. But, let's be honest; do you know of any woman who has never been accused of retail therapy? Like most women, I have been guilty of doing my fair share of shopping, but never at the expense of the well-being of my family. I can, however, comprehend that from the outside looking in, one could have miscalculated my position. Even I could consider myself an emotional shopper when I look back. Hindsight is a great tool. As the images of my shopping sprees flit through my mind, I can see my adrenaline increasing; I can see the excitement on my face from the hunt of finding that perfect piece at bargain prices. I'm not too prideful to admit that I sometimes justified the purchases by convincing myself that I deserved it. You know what we ladies say: "I work hard every day and I deserve a little happiness." As special as I believed those moments were to my stability, I rarely took advantage of the opportunity unless I was confident the monthly expenses would not suffer; therefore, they were limited and few and far between. However, I do remorsefully admit that during that same period, I used the needs of my children to avoid buying into the "save for retirement" concept. At my age, no one thinks about pensions and annuities. My response was more geared towards the idea that "nobody has time for that right now". Oh, to be so young and naive. I shake my head as I recall saying things like "I don't even know if I am going to live that long, so what's the point? Enjoy life while you can, girl." I think of this statement today and wonder who this person is, because that has got to be one of the most unintelligent statements for a woman with minor children to make. The welfare of my children could have potentially been at stake; unfortunately, I didn't realize it at the time. I should have given more thought to securing my financial future, which I later found out is more difficult as you get older. Despite my ignorance, please don't write me off too fast. I wasn't totally negligent. Periodically, I would put aside a few extra coins for that rainy day our mothers always insisted was right around the corner. However, despite all these presumed safeguards, I was blindsided by the course of events that shook my financial stability.

For reasons beyond my control, what seemed like just another ordinary Thursday turned out to be one of the most pivotal moments of my life. My thoughts gradually shifted into overdrive, challenging me to consider whether my modest spending habits contributed in the slightest way to my financial demise. However, the evidence proved otherwise. The communication deficiency between my husband and me, along with the shabby way the separation unfolded and the divorce itself, were all key factors that played major roles in securing my economic pitfall. The aftermath of that day left me speechless. I was faced with the added responsibility of picking up all the broken pieces of my life and my sons' lives. At the time, my boys were less than five years old.

As I envisioned the uncertainty of my financial future, I became perplexed by my husband's actions. I remember him asking "How in the world did we get here?" as if I were responsible for the destruction confronting us. I was in disbelief as to how any of my actions warranted this type of insensitive treatment. Did I not deserve a conversation prior to the rolling out of his events? We both knew that paying our bills on time was a priority. Our financial obligations went in this order: mortgage, car notes, the electricity bill, and food. At that time, paying the minimum on our credit cards sounded like a great idea until I learned about interest rates. I was a stickler about credit because I understood that in America you may not have money but, if you have good credit, you can pretty much buy anything. I found comfort in the thought that if these areas were maintained, life was good. Saving for the future was a gray area for us with all our expenditures, especially the disbursements related to our sons. I was constantly trying to find ways to improve. It relieved me to know that by being aware of the ratio of debt to earnings we still managed to maintain a sense of financial reconciliation.

Bracing myself as I cautiously drift back to that period of my life, I can still remember the hurt, pain and embarrassment I felt. It was so severely heart-wrenching that it almost felt surreal. Although the painful sting has since dissolved, the memories are still unpleasantly difficult to recall. In retrospect, those thoughts reminded me of a time when life could only be summed up in two little words: cruel and unfair. My thoughts painted pictures of my past that I wasn't quite ready to digest. Yet, as much as I tried to deny it, that was my reality. My life had taken on a different direction I thought would never resurface. I was a single parent again, and I was now accountable for the next chain of events. Even though I felt like my position in this dilemma was never considered, the sensitive and unspoken question was released into the atmosphere: What did I do that was so dreadfully wrong? Simultaneously, the images of the bank account with a balance I did not expect flashed through my brain. As the reflection became vivid, the account that once showed hope was now depleted. How was I going to survive without any financial assistance? The monthly obligations flooded my mind, provoking an intense and unfiltered conversation with God. Without emitting a sound, my lips formed the words "Dear God, this cannot be real; you have got to be kidding me. Surely, you can see that this burden is far too great for me to handle alone. In case you forgot, let me remind you of my current employment status; it's part-time with zero benefits. Jesus, you do see these two small, blameless children who will be depending on me to meet all their necessities, don't you? This cannot be what you meant for my life." I closed my eyes and concentrated with difficulty on my breathing, attempting to slow it down as I inaudibly uttered the words "Jesus, please!" For the first time in my life I openly admitted that I was beyond angry at God. I was raging on the inside, yet my exterior posture was calm. I couldn't understand how He could allow this to happen to me and my two guiltless sons. I was furious, and I wondered whether God was truly as kind and loving as I had once understood Him to be. If indeed He was God, this didn't resemble love or kindness at any magnitude. I stopped myself short of rejecting my belief in God, because somewhere deep down inside I knew I would be crossing a serious line with dangerous repercussions. I also knew my craziness was getting the better of me by attempting to manipulate my situation as if it was God's fault. I also knew hell was too high of a price for me to pay for my temporary insanity. Additionally, within the confines of my heart, I had already acknowledged that God was real on more than a few occasions. Every time I uttered the name of Jesus, and whenever I asked for help, it was a sure sign that I believed in him. But at this point, I needed to release the pain I was feeling inside. I needed the anguish to reside somewhere other than in the depths of my soul. I had history of what being in His Presence could do. I knew if I could only get into the posture of worship, God would release something for me to receive hope, despite broadcasting my wrath with little concern about the repercussions. The condition of my heart was hardening. Had this situation only affected me, I believe it would have been much easier for me to digest the injustice. The well-thought-out plan was the reason why my life changed so fast, so unexpectedly. Nothing in my power could change my predicament. I was unnerved, because it wasn't just about me. Everyone of importance to me would experience the aftermath of this pain.

Defeat was starting to sink in and I had no clue how to stop it. Shaking myself, I pondered the information circling around in my head. Was it not our God-given responsibility to provide for the welfare of our children or, at a minimum, for their safety and security? How could God allow this to happen? They are innocent children. Laboring to prevent the tears from falling again, I struggled internally to come to grips with the events that were transpiring. I was in shock and my responses were all over place, making absolutely no sense. So many things were coming against me that I had no solutions as the fiasco continued to evolve. What had I allowed to slip through the cracks, unnoticed? Was I reaping something I didn't even know I had sowed? It appeared as if I were having an out-of-body experience. I am sure it was due to my denial of the circumstances, yet it was unquestionably very real. I was confused as to the way this situation was unraveling. I kept trying to bargain with God: "Please help me; assure me that this thing I'm experiencing is just some awful terrifying nightmare. Please reduce the probing pain burning within my heart and put an end to my suffering. Please let life as I once knew it return to normal." Unfortunately, what I so desperately yearned for did not happen. None of my emotional bursts were satisfied. All I could do was let go. I curled up into the fetal position and sobbed until I no longer produced tears. At some point, I remember having just enough energy to pick myself up to get into my car. I drove around the Beltway in circles with no destination in mind. I was merely driving around aimlessly in an attempt to escape from the pain I was feeling. I wanted to just give up. This thing was way too unbearable, and now all that was visible too; I was a failure. For the first few days after my foundation was shaken, I wished I could have ended it all. I thought about ways I could exit out of my misery with the least amount of resistance. I debated getting into my car and driving until I either ran out of road, gas, or found myself in a place where nobody knew my name. I was in so much pain. Going through these possibilities was the only way for me to avoid the elephant in my life that I would one day have to confront, but this wasn't the day. I questioned whether there was truly purpose behind this dreadful pain. Rather than dwell on that notion, I switched gears and headed to another dark place, mentally. I convinced myself that doing good doesn't matter. If you do good, you still end up getting hurt, so why even put forth the effort? My only saving grace at that uncertain time was with my two sons, who were observing this madness. Their love for me was the driving force as to why giving up was not an option for me. They were all that I had. They were valuable, and I owed it to them to provide the best life possible, regardless of the circumstances staring me in the face. After all, never once did they ask to be here; that was my choice.

The consequences of that day changed the course of my life forever, both emotionally and financially. For as long as I can remember, I wasn't one to misuse or mishandle money; I had to work too hard to get my share of the pie. I understood that money was the necessary means to acquire things that would ultimately benefit my family. In the long term, the assets from the purchases would produce a peaceful home and a beautiful environment for us all to flourish. There were no hidden agendas, or at least that is what I assumed. I believed that once the "I dos" were said, that what was mine was his and what was his was mine, good, bad or indifferent. I had no financial secrets. There were no secret off-shore accounts or concealed domestic bank accounts, for that matter. However, on that day I learned how one transaction, orchestrated by the hands of the person who pledged to love me through the highs and the low times, wiped out the account our family depended upon to live. To make matters worse, I had no access to the funds required to resolve the financial climate I had inherited. That entire scenario later nearly destroyed my creditability. My credit score was like an embarrassing joke. Bill collectors were constantly calling, and the only mail I received was from creditors. For months I felt defenseless, ashamed and embarrassed. I must confess that the ordeal lasted far longer than I would have preferred. In fact, the initial rebuilding phase started in my late twenties and it felt like it took a lifetime for me to bounce back. However, the lessons learned proved to me that God is the one and only true source for everything I have in my life. After coming to terms with my situation, I understood how extreme measures are often the best teachers. As unwarranted as we think they are, those are the lessons that prepared me to do great things for God in excellence. I learned the true value of obedience, patience and sacrifice.

Due to my major financial mishap, I was placed into a position that forced me to create a financial plan to achieve my **financial** goals. Settling for my current condition was not viable or worthwhile for my future. I developed a strategic plan that would afford me the opportunity to be self-sufficient so that I could care for our two minor children effectively. The plan helped me to set my direction and establish priorities to avoid making costly monetary mistakes in the future. This plan sounds good but trust me; the to-do-list did not produce an overnight success for me to regain my financial stability. It was more like an extensive fifteen-year journey with lots of ups and downs and in-betweens. My unwillingness to take ownership of my predicament is what initially hindered the process. However, I did outlive the debt crisis that once plagued my life by using God's blueprint as my guide. Instead of being a slave to money, God taught me how to be a master of money. The process started slowly; at first, I prayed and asked God for direction. I needed to build up my confidence in Him before embarking on this new venture. I also needed His mercy for so many reasons, including the pride, unforgiveness, anger, bitterness and the coldness dwelling inside my heart that also ruled my soul. Thankfully, I regained my mind, I realized and admitted that I never even asked God if my choices were in His will for my life. Being honest, I had to acknowledge that my anger towards God was more about being angry at myself for the undisciplined decisions I had made that almost ruined my life. I was the reason for my confusion, not God. Once I accepted and took ownership of my shortcomings and mistakes, I gradually became uncluttered and free. I sensed that my hope was on the rise again.

I started researching and studying the word of God to see what He had to say about money. 1 Timothy 6:10 Amplified Bible (AMP) leaped out at me for various reasons, but mostly because I had heard several variations of the meaning of this scripture. I really desired to know God's take on this verse. So, I decided to read it for myself to hear the words from my own mouth. As I read, "For the love of money [that is, the greedy desire for it and the willingness to gain it unethically] is a root of all sorts of evil, and some by longing for it have wandered away from the faith and pierced themselves [through and through] with many sorrows." My prior understanding was being challenged, which made it a must for me to read the passage out loud again to make sure my ears were not playing tricks on me. I guess that is why I now have a fond appreciation for 2 Timothy 2:15 Amplified Bible (AMP). It tells us "study and do your best to present yourself to God approved, a workman [tested by trial] who has no reason to be ashamed, accurately handling and skillfully teaching the word of truth." My inner voice made me pay attention, as the major difference between what the actual scripture says versus what people who lack understanding was exposed. What is commonly claimed about this verse is that money is the root of all evil. The scripture is not stating that at all; the actual scripture says, "For the love of money is a root of all kinds of evil." If only I had a dollar for the countless times the improper meaning has been recanted, I would be one wealthy woman. Based on the counterfeit description, we have all been led at one time or another to believe that money is evil. Let me clear that improper thought out of your mind; money doesn't have that kind of control on its own. On the contrary; when we make money an idol in our lives, we are choosing to let it regulate us. We must recognize that wealth is morally neutral: there is nothing wrong with money, in and of itself, or with the ownership of money. However, when money begins to control us, rest assured that trouble is most definitely hovering close by. We must never forget that money is simply a resource or a tool, just like our gifts and talents, whose proper functions are to expand the Kingdom of God. Matthew 6:19-21 Amplified

Bible (AMP) makes it clear by saying, "[Do] not store up for yourselves [material] treasures on earth, where moth and rust destroy, and where thieves break in and steal. But store up for yourselves treasures in heaven, where neither moth nor rust destroys and where thieves do not break in and steal; for where your treasure is, there your heart [your wishes, your desires; that on which your life centers] will be also." So, I had to ask myself the difficult question, "Where is my treasure?" If it is truly God, am I doing what we are told to do in Matthew 6:33 Amplified Bible (AMP)? "But first and most importantly seek (aim at, strive after) His kingdom and His righteousness [His way of doing and being right—the attitude and character of God], and all these things will be given to you also."

Thankfully, I was able to comprehend this truth about God, money and its purpose to create some new habits to assist with my financial goals. I refused to buy into the enemy's shenanigans, which shined a bright light on poverty as if it is a badge of honor to be poor. Trust me; it is okay to believe in God and have money. It is not a cardinal sin. Common sense tells me that it takes money to do the work of the Lord here on earth. Yet, to advance the cause, a fair share of believers refuse to surrender their purse strings. I often sit back and wonder whether we really believe that a project of this enormity - advancing the kingdom of God - will not require some sort of financial support from every believer, wealthy or not. Or perhaps people's issues are like mine used to be: the trap that convinces them that they are unusable by God. If financial freedom was going to be possible for me, I had to be willing to do whatever was necessary to overcome this hurdle. I needed God to know that I could be trusted. I wanted the first part of

Luke 16:10 Amplified Bible (AMP) to be my truth, not the later part. "He who is faithful in a very little thing is also faithful in much; and He who is dishonest in a very little thing is also dishonest in much." I had already read the passage in the book of Proverbs that told me poverty and disgrace come to him who ignores instruction. I had no desire to be poor or a disgrace, so I focused on following instructions. Where could I find instructions I could follow? That was easy; I found them in Matthew 7:7-11 Amplified Bible (AMP). It tells me to ask and keep on asking, and it will be given to you; seek and keep on seeking, and you will find; knock *and* keep on knocking, and the door will be opened to you. For everyone who keeps on asking receives, and He who keeps on seeking finds, and to Him who keeps on knocking, it will be opened. "Or what man is there among you who, if his son asks for bread, will [instead] give Him a stone? Or if He asks for a fish, will [instead] give Him a snake? If you then, evil (sinful by nature) as you are, know how to give good and advantageous gifts to your children, how much more will your Father who is in heaven [perfect as He is] give what is good and advantageous to those who keep on asking Him." Being in lack no longer worked for me. I submitted to the urge to press towards the mark. So, I started asking, knocking and seeking. Again, I asked God the question, "Why not me?" I was available, despite being weary and depleted. I no longer wanted to align with the "why me" or "what if" syndromes that formerly governed my life. I did not want to be like the people I read about in the Bible or repeat the reluctant habits of the people surrounding me, who aborted their destiny because of fear and a lack of resources. I didn't want to misrepresent God; I wanted my light to shine so brightly that the universe would notice. I wanted to accomplish all that He put in me. I wanted to fulfill every assignment entrusted to me. I continued searching my bible for clarity, for the mind is a powerful tool when it is fully focused. I craved being a caretaker of God's assets, understanding that when done incorrectly, it will cause the demise of destiny and purpose.

Of course, the timeframe I needed to accomplish the improvement of my financial outlook was tight, and the remedy was much more difficult than I had calculated. Instilling the application to regain my financial stance was somewhat problematic. Daily, I had to literally coach myself with the newfound treasure of information I was acquiring. I had to be willing to confidently confront potential money risks that had the potential to jeopardize the rebounding financial advancement I was working towards. The completion of my launched goals was a must. To be a meticulous manager over the money God entrusts to me is challenging and demanding because of my compassion for others. By not addressing specific issues, I could in theory increase the unforeseen deathtraps threatening my financial survival if I was not careful. I had to learn how to draw the line when it came to money with significant others, family members, close friends and charitable donations in order to avoid hostile disagreements, tension, and resentment. At times I was reluctant. It was quite taxing when some problems were not easily resolved, especially when the wisdom of how to handle money was in the forefront of my heart. My ability to maintain the proper level of biblical attributes was essential if my financial outlook was going to improve.

As I continued navigating through the process of re-building my financial wealth, staying focused, designating uninterrupted study time, and paying attention to the major and minor details while upholding my patience was not a game. If I truly wanted to see the manifested promises, maintaining these aspects was mandatory. Once my calculated plan was in operation, my concentration went into creating a workable realistic budget while rebuilding my credit score. In my study time, I became quite knowledgeable about the benefits of an ecstatic giver and its connection to wealth and favor. One of the hardest things to do in life is to do the right thing all the time, especially concerning finances. So instead of looking to society for the right answers, Malachi, chapter 3 10:12 provided me with some insight. These verses captured my attention because, on any given Sunday, they are the most recurring passages spoken at the pulpit concerning giving. I like the way Malachi 3:10-12 Amplified Bible (AMP) breaks down this passage: "Bring all the tithes (the tenth) into the storehouse, so that there may be food in My house, and test Me now in this,' says the Lord of hosts, 'if I will not open for you the windows of heaven and pour out for you [so great] a blessing until there is no more room to receive it. Then I will rebuke the devourer (insects, plague) for your sake and He will not destroy the fruits of the ground, nor will your vine in the field drop its grapes [before harvest],' says the Lord of hosts. 'All nations shall call you happy and blessed, for you shall be a land of delight,' says the Lord of hosts.'" As you can see, the rewards for giving outrank the penalties for not giving by far. With knowledge comes understanding. In prior years, I would have considered myself to be a decent tither, but decent and consistent have two very different meanings. So, there was room for improvement for me, especially when my money got a little funny. By "funny", I mean "mismanaged", because I fell into that trap, as well. You know the one where the money marked for God seems to be used for something else on Saturday before church on Sunday. I must be honest: there were times I would forego giving tithes, and I justified my actions by saying God understands that I just want to be a good mother. I found it difficult to choose between purchasing the necessities and the incidentals like birthday presents or low-budget entertainment for my kids or giving God His due. A gut feeling would remind me of the powerful reasons for doing the right thing, yet I found myself doing what was familiar by succumbing to unbelief, never quite understanding that my sacrifices would be an indication of my devotion to God. Those tough decisions proved that my faith in God as my provider digressed. I am sure it wasn't necessary for us to eat out, even if it was just McDonald's. I am sure we didn't have to go to the movies, even if it was just the matinee, and I am pretty sure I didn't have to buy that new pair of shoes on sale that I truly did not need, just because the sale would end before my next payday. It all boiled down to my not having confidence in God to provide for us. I thought it was best for me to take matters into my own hands. This response only legitimized my fears while sabotaging my faith, until I got sick and tired of always coming up short. I had to learn how to resist the negative comments being publicly shared; the ones proclaiming that all pastors misuse the money given to the church for their own personal gain; the ones broadcasting that they use the church money to buy fancy houses, expensive cars and name brand clothing when their members are living without simple necessities.

I couldn't allow myself to subscribe to the negativity being presented by those who lacked understanding of the things of God. The truth of the matter is there is no absolute anything, other than God. Sure, there are some pastors who may abuse their power, but not all pastors are dishonest. Just like not all people are immoral, there are some, but not all. I needed to hold on to what I knew to be true; that the God I serve is more than able to deal with those who distort the gospel for personal gain. It was not my responsibility to judge, nor was this my battle to fight. What I was accountable for was not letting these kinds of distractions impact how I honor God. The alarm didn't go off immediately, but when it did, I understood that God does not want or need any of my money. Currency is not required in heaven. But what is required is my desire to leverage my earthly resources for the kingdom.

It took a few years for me to fully accept the wisdom associated with the importance of consistent giving. His teachings were showing me why trusting an unseen God may be difficult, especially concerning money, but when I do I will excel at the undertaking of overseeing the assets delegated to me by God. I was discovering God's ways don't always make sense. However, what did make sense - the obligations, the responsibilities and promises - I could expect when partnering with God. I was in far too deep to quit now; in addition, my love for God was increasing, which made me determined to keep His commands. I must confess, I don't always get this right, but I refuse to stay down. Every day that His breath freely flows throughout my spirit I vow to present the best version of myself to the universe.

Of course, waiting for the great return is difficult and unnatural because we live in a microwave society that has convinced us to expect everything instantly. I had to deliberately remind myself that just because something has not fully manifested and results aren't visible to the human eye, it doesn't mean there is no growth. Think of the time it takes a planted seed to sprout. Remember the process it must endure: light must be provided, the temperature must be stable, and you must water it regularly. Even after doing all these things, you still must wait to see growth, and you must have faith to believe that something is happening under the surface. As you continue to water the seed and allow the sun to nurture it, eventually fruit is produced. The same principle is true with regard to financial matters. In the height of these moments, fear and procrastination would often rear its ugly head to outshine my progress. I had to do a complete mind overhaul, trashing the unqualified material that had proven to be worthless and replacing the previously occupied space with applicable biblical principles.

After countless debates with myself, the next hurdle demanding my attention was how to confidently ask questions regarding finances when our culture considers the act as impolite. It's not as if I was asking strangers, however. I wanted to ask those with whom I had fostered relationships. After all, they had already proven that they knew what was an asset and what was a liability, so why reinvent a roadmap when someone I respected had already traveled that road? I decided to ignore pride and ego and forged ahead. Like they say on Wall Street, no financial affiliation is exempt; risks are always involved. I hit this barrier head on and gave myself permission to be completely open concerning my financial position, while hoping they would reciprocate. I was praying that they could educate me by passing on some of their financial knowledge, focusing on how to avoid costly economic mistakes and ways to increase my financial portfolio. I studied those around me who were proficient in wealth to assist in my financial planning. I figured I had already hit rock bottom and my financial credit worthiness was already questionable, so I had everything to gain at this point. I refused to be victimized by my condition. This situation forced me to examine myself to see if I had what it took to change my position. Change can be scary, especially when you know the required concentrated effort needed to produce great change, but I accepted the challenge nervously. I made God and the things important to God a priority by being a faithful tither. What I also noticed was that when you give out of obligation or begrudgingly, you abort the blessings attached to giving. God wants us to be excited and cheerful when giving to expand His work on earth. He doesn't want us to give out of tradition or, for that matter, to give a certain amount out of obligation to satisfy our own conscience. No; He wants to know that we will not waiver when asked to generously share of whatever talents, abilities, or wealth He has assigned to us. I question whether we do ourselves a disservice by not seeing beyond the law requiring a tenth to be dedicated back to God. I believe in tithing, but why hinder the hand of God by solely focusing on just tithing ten percent. Wake up! God's pockets are much deeper than ten percent. Imagine being able to support the expansion of the Kingdom of God at a rate surpassing the controversial ten percent tithe. That is the legacy of giving I want for myself, my children and my children's children, having confidence that when I cheerfully give without limits, God can trust me even the more. This was a major factor in my recovery progression: recognizing wealth as a gift entrusted to me from God that I must be willing to share generously with the less fortunate and to carry out His work on earth.

So, once I was unwavering with giving to God, I implemented some of the advice of my friends and associates who are successful in this area and I started investing in myself. It was difficult at first to pay myself, especially when the bills were mounting up, but my vision was not based on where I was at the time. I was looking ahead, knowing that the "pay myself" account would one day be the account I use to fund my purpose. It took dedication, discipline, and consistency to stay true to the plan but once I was fully committed to giving God what is His and paying myself, there was no stopping me. I opened three separate bank accounts; not all at once and not all at the same bank, however. At first, I had very little money to deposit in each of the accounts, but I stayed true to the strategy. I gave myself a target amount to reach and once I surpassed the pre-determined balance, I would transfer the overage into the three accounts at the different banks. This is a process I still practice today.

I labeled one of the accounts "short term", because it is used for the unexpected emergencies that we don't anticipate. You know the ones: they are when you suddenly need new tires, the washing machine breaks down, or grown children call needing a little support every now and then.

The second account is my travel account. I use the funds in this account to give myself a nice vacation every year. God requires us to take care of our temples, a/k/a our bodies, and the only way to achieve great results is to periodically disengage from the routine and go somewhere to be refreshed. It is imperative that you occasionally make yourself a priority in order to remain in a healthy place where you can add value to those connected to you.

The third account I opened was a money market account. This account was for the purposes of securing my financial stability for my golden years to supplement the pension benefits being offered at my place of employment. I was becoming a full-fledged, active CFO of my life. Through the years, I have been blessed to have resources that permit me to add stocks and certificates to my portfolio; so, as you can see, I am always learning.

On the flip side, the debt I had incurred had to be tackled. By having debt, I did not understand at the time that I was creating it; that all I was doing was simply borrowing from the money I hoped to earn in the future. This only kept me from accomplishing my financial goals. It was difficult, but sacrifices had to be made if I was going to pull myself out of this hole. I could not allow my circumstances to deter me from my obligations. I contacted my creditors, explained my situation, and made payment arrangements I could handle. If, for some unforeseen reason I had a problem not making a payment, I contacted them. I took responsibility and they didn't have to chase me down. Once that was completed, any extra income, i.e. tax refunds or rebate checks, went to pay off the credit cards with the least balance, and it didn't matter if the extra was only five dollars. Five dollars makes a difference - just ask a mother who has no lunch money for her kid.

Once I paid off the initial credit card, I took the funds that would have gone towards paying that card and applied it to the next card on my list. Seeing "paid in full" on an account was the best encouragement I could have gotten to continue. They may have been small amounts to begin with, but they were gone - wiped off my credit. I felt good about myself, and my debt elimination future seemed probable, with visible progress being made. After paying off several bills, my credit score changed. This put me in position to take advantage of some of the zero interest credit cards offers I was receiving in the mail. I transferred the balances owed to a new credit card with no interest and vowed to pay off the balance before the interest rates were adjusted. Be careful with this option, you must have a realistic plan for this window of opportunity, because interests rates go up considerably after the promotion period. I did not deviate from the calculated amount; it was the amount owed divided by the number of paychecks I would receive during the allotted period. I put vacations, entertainment, eating out and shopping sprees on pause. This move revealed that I was an emotional shopper. I used shopping as my coping mechanism to avoid dealing with uncomfortable situations and deep-rooted emotions that I viewed as out of my control. I knew I couldn't live the life I desired if I didn't get to the root of this problem, so I found a therapist and sat on her couch until results were visible. That was one of the best decisions I ever made.

In the end, my willingness to do what was necessary, made it all worth it. Peace and harmony were restored. I can still remember the day I walked into one of my favorite stores and came out without a purchase: talk about being empowered! I no longer pretend to be somebody else when my phone rings, fearing that it is a bill collector, and disappointment and anxiety no longer constrain me when it comes time to pay my monthly bills. I also have learned how to use wisdom and not my emotions when folks ask to borrow money. Unfortunately, people tend to look at the exterior of my life and draw their own conclusions when they have no clue as to my reality. The beam in my eyes that people see is the measurement they use to predetermine my bank account status. They are great at making assumptions about my money for their hardships. Of course, when their expectations aren't met, they become angry without any thoughts of their own selfish motives. I am really honest in asking the tough questions - especially to myself. If the loan is granted and never repaid, will it negatively impact my finances? If the answer is yes, I say no. This is extremely tough for me, because I empathize with people and, innately, I want to help. I have learned how to exercise caution, because people will try to manipulate you until you end up broke. Only my inner circle would know if things are not going so well. They look beyond my facial expressions and appearance. They know me. These are the individuals who have taken the time to care about Lisa and my well-being, and not my bank account.

So, as I reflect on my financial journey, the nervousness associated with my accumulated **deficit,** the consequences of unrealistic financial choices and mismanagement of personal funds were key elements that drove me to discover the principles of wealth. However, by my obtaining the necessary skills to precisely manage and cultivate my money to generate optimistic returns, I found out that when followed obediently, God's plan works. Since I am no longer angry at God for allowing the financial travesty to occur, I appreciate Romans

8:28, the Amplified Bible (AMP): "and we know [with great confidence] that God [who is deeply concerned about us] causes all things to work together [as a plan] for good for those who love God, to those who are called according to His plan and purpose." I am so profoundly amazed at Christ's love for me during my darkest periods of life. I was able to make peace with the entire ordeal as God reestablishes my worth. I accepted my being out-of-focus as a contributing factor in my financial downfall and the rage and bitterness I felt towards the person who initiated the plan that affected my financial foundation. Now, when I glance back over my life, I no longer question why I had to endure such an undesirable process to discover my true potential. Instead, I am thankful for the long suffering of God's love. I am grateful for Hebrews 12:6 Amplified Bible (AMP): "For the Lord disciplines and corrects those whom He loves, and He punishes every son whom He receives and welcomes [to His heart]." Remember what I said earlier; His ways are not our ways. When I think about my actions, which deserved a much harsher penalty, God's Grace intervened. During those moments of temporary insanity when I chose my wants, my ambitions, my desires and my goals, which all included some form of toxic or unhealthy agent, His love never wavered. My bank accounts are not at the bare minimum anymore. There has been no famine-like season in my finances for quite a while, because I refuse to allow lack to rule. Having not reached the capacity of my purpose, I know I have only scratched the surface of the financial success available to me. So, I continue to find comfort in knowing that God only funds His vision, and I am expecting God to rock my world financially, not because I am worthy, but because He has searched me and found me to be trustworthy, authentic, consistent, compassionate and one who has proven that when life gets difficult, His belief in me shows up, making me an informant of both wealth and the ability to create wealth.

chapter 7

Marriage

Romantic movies, love songs and romance novels all have one thing in common: they promote marriage as desirable, easy-going, happy, and a must-have for every woman. So, I thought it would have been a seamless fit for me. After all, as a teenager, I believed that marriage was one great big romance filled with adventure and excitement, laughter, tears of joy and love, just like in the movies. I would be so completely stunned by the impressive ways the characters showed strong feelings of affection to one another that it would bring tears to my eyes. It all seemed so real, even though many of the storylines were fictional. My enthusiasm level was so high, I felt like the cast and I were knitted together. The uplifting experiences of watching the happily-ever-after endings took my breath away. Love movies had the power to propel my emotional stimulation from zero to one hundred in a matter of seconds; not to mention the fact that as a teen I thought that if I mimicked what I saw being expressed, I would obtain the same results in my own personal life. If you were a romance junky like me, maybe you too can remember those images I am referring to - the ones of married couples spending quality time together filled with countless romantic dinners and long walks on the beach while watching the sunset or the sunrise; the ones in which the couples went on dreamy getaways and always seemed to be engaged in profound conversations with each other that often led to mind-blowing sex. The couples were rarely seen arguing and if by chance they did argue, the disagreements were minor and ended with a kiss as they made up. This helped me envision my future with a husband who would be willing to do everything in his power to please me; my very own prince charming. In return, I would be a Superwoman of a wife and people would be in awe of the love we shared. Hook, line and sinker, I bought into this dream, never paying any attention to the fact that there were no valley encounters or ordinary days between the couples. My perception of marriage was so high school and juvenile that it is mind-blowing to me just how inexperienced and immature I was. In the end, it turned out to be incredibly harmful. I truly believe that my approach towards marriage was the stimulus for the downfall of my failed marriages and my being an underachiever in romantic relationships. It is unbelievable to me, knowing the woman that I am now, that I considered romantic movies, love songs and romance novels as great foundations for building a successful marriage. Don't judge me; it's more common than you think. The power of a two-hour love movie can underwrite your key relationships if you are not careful. I shiver when I hear the words, "I now pronounce you husband and wife", because those words remind me of all my infractions.

Due to my undeveloped mentality, I preserved far too many pointless influences that tried to control and manipulate my thoughts and decisions regarding marriage. So much so that they became giant distractions to persuade me that a godly marriage was not meant for me, and that a godly husband was not in the cards for someone like me. Instead of trusting God, I allowed my insecurities to control my desires. I turned my back on purpose and slowly drifted towards things of no relevance. I put a lot of effort into responding to worldly, ill-defined, nonspecific marital relationships. I got a husband, but it sure wasn't the one God created for me. He wasn't my Prince Charming. I was more consumed with the wedding than the marriage. Thinking about what our principal responsibilities would be to each other wasn't even on my radar. It didn't even cross my mind that my actions should assist my spouse in fulfilling destiny and reaching his full potential. Speaking from my own perspective, my interests were selfish in nature. I was petty and outspoken to a fault with my opinions about everything. I was so out of touch with reality that I convinced myself that we had no real design flaws that needed fixing prior to our formal "I do" ceremony. The sad reality is that neither one of us had a clue as to how to build a successful, godly marriage. I don't recall ever having any serious conversations about our expectations as a married couple prior to walking down the aisle. The only things we focused on were that we enjoyed each other's company, we were attracted to each other, both of us were legally employed, and that we had our own homes to lay our heads down in that didn't belong to our parents, while the jury had not yet determined if we could even be best friends.

What I quickly learned in this union was that romantic movies, love songs and romance novels do not offer you the proper advice or path to follow when your marriage falls apart unexpectedly. Like the other areas of my life, I was discovering that there are practical and impractical principles to marriage I didn't anticipate. The cycle of life was heavy for me, going from being single, to an unwed mother, to married with a child, to married with children, and then to divorce. I struggled endlessly with trying to figure out who I was and my place in the world.

At some point, if you are not careful, your faith will diminish if you are not watchful. When the direction of my life changed unexpectedly, and I found myself in uncharted territory, I felt scared, alone and lost. My faith took a big dive as it started to fade. The uncertainty of not knowing exactly where this new path was leading weighed me down. I found out quickly that marriage, just like nature, has a vast array of seasons. I was also finding out, though not as quickly, that marriage can be stifled by romance novels, great love songs and romantic movies, because of unrealistic expectations about how your spouse should love you. I had yet to discover the passage in 1st Corinthians 13:7-8 Amplified Bible (AMP): "Love bears all things [regardless of what comes], believes all things [looking for the best in each one], hopes all things [remaining steadfast during difficult times], endures all things [without weakening]. Love never fails [it never fades nor ends]."

I was unprepared for those winter seasons that required me to provide the kind of love found in 1st Corinthians, chapter 13 - especially for the lengthy amount of time my marriages seem to settle in the "winter season"; talk about cold! Because I did not do my due diligence prior to yelling the word "yes" with excitement and enthusiasm, I had to suck it up and hope for the best. I didn't understand that when the temperature drops in the relationship, it's God's signal to let us know that some extra tender loving care is needed if a strong marriage is indeed what we are seeking. But I was clueless to the signs, and because we didn't take the time to reveal to each other what we already knew about ourselves, all the wake-up calls were ignored. Negotiating our differences was far too much work. So, like most of us do when we don't know how to address an uncomfortable subject, we retreated to separate corners in hopes that it would just work itself out. Well; signing the divorce papers taught me that it *doesn't* just work itself out.

After my initial divorce, I totally convinced myself that there was no distinction between being married and exclusively dating someone. I validated my actions by telling myself that if the relationship was unsuccessful, we could just move on. It was too great of a risk to expect permanency. My exit strategy had already been pre-determined. Countless times I ran the escape route drills in my head, so I was always prepared. To finalize the end for me only required a quick conversation with ambiguous details. I would throw in a few sentences about how I had a lot on my plate, making it very clear that my children and my work are priorities and that there was nothing we could do to salvage the relationship. In my dysfunctional brain I was being a martyr. In reality, however, I was only saving myself from the possibility of being hurt. I was satisfied with my convictions, or so I thought; unconsciously, though, I was only letting my pain rule my heart. I chose to settle for what appeared to be safe rather than what was best for me, because that would require effort and discipline on my part. I wasn't ready to fully commit to doing the necessary work to become that healthy, present, full of life partner who would someday attract someone deserving of that 1st Corinthians kind of love.

I was tired and frustrated, with no clue as to where to start to rebuild myself or my life. Obstacles like these only forced me to put up all kinds of barriers that provided me with a false sense of protection. I had walls that blocked out unwanted feelings, walls to keep distance between me and unwanted intimate relationships, and walls to hide my insecurities. The effects of this were visible in all my relationships, yet I still chose to turn a blind eye to my own contribution to the dysfunction. The effects of my failed marriages paralyzed me in more ways than one. Physically, emotionally, financially and spiritually; in my heart of hearts, I convinced myself that I was wounded and damaged beyond repair.

For years I continued on this downward spiral, believing God didn't love me because I had committed one of the ultimate sins and got a divorce on more than one occasion. I suffered in silence feeling ashamed, rejected, unloved and unworthy. I was also feeling guilty over my other unhealthy decisions, which included worrying about the wedding itself instead of worrying about things of substance, such as asking for marital guidance. I chose to focus on my dress, the colors of the dresses for my bridal party, our rings, the honeymoon and all the special things that transpire on the wedding day itself. As far as I can recall, I don't believe I gave any attention to what would happen after the wedding day. The "us" being paraded around on our wedding day was all I envisioned. All of my attention was focused upon making that day beautiful for all our family and friends who would be in attendance. I put more value on the appearance of my life rather than on the true condition of my heart. I never once took the time to ask whether this was what God desired for my life. I couldn't answer the question if I was genuinely pleased with the person with whom I had agreed to share the rest of my life. Rather than struggle with this issue, I deliberated on what I felt was controllable and what I believed everyone whose opinion I valued expected for my life. At the time, from my perspective, I never sensed that I was safe or secure enough in any of my friendships to discuss my apprehensions or failures and how they made me feel as a woman or, for that matter, as a human being. I often felt as if I were under a magnifying glass and there was not a judgement-free zone available to me to express my insecurities, weaknesses or fears. I was slowly suffocating with no visible life support in sight. My heart had hardened because of the sufferings I had endured. For the record, my perception of marriage was not always so jaded. I strongly believed in the sacredness of marriage, or at least of what I knew about it. It sounds so bizarre now, knowing the person I have developed into.

Unfortunately, for most of my thirty something years I was so far off base when it came to the purpose of marriage that it was scary. That is, until I started studying the word of God for myself. My heart was starting to glow again. I completely understand now why a lack of knowledge is why we perish; revelation is a powerful weapon. I found out that God does not categorize sin, which helped me find a way to recover from the stigma of divorce. This doesn't mean that God gave me a free pass to continue being a repeat offender of divorce, but He did show me that I still had a future, because of the blood He shed on the cross. In the eyes of God, we have all fallen short of His glory. I found out that His love truly does cover us all. His undying love for me in my broken condition gave me the courage to accept the healing process I so desperately needed to be whole again. I willingly acknowledge my errors and ask for forgiveness with the help of 1st John 1:9 Amplified Bible (AMP): "If we [freely] admit that we have sinned and confess our sins, He is faithful and just [true to His own nature and promises], and will forgive our sins and cleanse us continually from all unrighteousness [our wrongdoing, everything not in conformity with His will and purpose]", which helped me overcome many strong holds. I decided right then and there that I no longer wanted to live a life filled with rejection and pain, so I decided to trust God completely. This was a first for me. There was no doubt in my request; I truly believed it was all possible for me. Finally, I could let go off all my past hurts, insecurities and feelings of hopelessness. I held on tightly to God's love and grace because I knew I was only in the initial stages of the healing process. I also discovered that real change was possible and there was a blueprint for me follow. Acts 3:19 Amplified Bible (AMP) tells us to repent [change our inner selves—our old ways of thinking, regret past sins] and return [to God—seek His purpose for our lives], so that our sins may be wiped away [blotted out, completely erased], so that times of refreshing may come from the presence of the Lord [restoring us like a cool wind on a hot day]. Now that's a miracle, when you experience such an unconventional love that is not physically driven. It made me remember all the times I wrestled with God, looking for a way out and a way to justify my fears by denouncing the importance of marriage. I remembered those moments when I questioned whether I would indeed go to hell if I entertained a relationship that permitted sex without marriage. God's word shut it all down. Instead of dealing with my requests the way I pictured, He showed me through His word how I was afraid of intimacy and being vulnerable. I wasn't sure I was up for this challenge. Thanks to God having His way in my life, and thanks to excellent Christian therapy, I am forever changed. I could sense my hope being restored. I no longer felt captive to my past, and my future was starting to look bright again.

Reflecting on those moments I realized that despite all the people who cared for me, no one ever took the time to explain to me the importance of a godly marriage. I don't know whether that was because they had no clue how to do it or whether they thought I would not listen. Either way, in the end, the blame fell on my shoulders. To be honest, I'm not even certain if the desire to truly know was apparent or if I even bothered to ask someone. You know what a made-up mind will do; it will do exactly what it wants to do no matter the outcome. A blurred and jacked-up vision will make you miss out on the great future God has prepared for you. It took my being sincerely truthful to myself to recognize my vital errors. I realized I didn't adopt this approach towards marriage and life based upon my own brilliance; instead, the approach materialized behind the actions of another person towards me. Someone neglected to have the marital breakup conversation with me during my early adult years, and that left me feeling powerless. So, to protect myself from ever experiencing this type of agony again, I vowed not to ever allow this to happen to me again. I would never subject myself to any relationship that required one hundred percent commitment of me and, ironically, I put God in this same category. Threats of risking it all were contained by the oversized, imaginary and impenetrable steel fence that surrounded my heart. At least, that is what I projected. Clearly, it was not obvious to me at that time that I was relinquishing my power into the hands of the individual who lacked creditability for the lifelong career to honor, love and protect me in the first place. However, this was my reality, which gave me a false sense of control. Divorced life had won; it shattered the authentic me. It persuaded me to align with the notion that a committed, long-term dating relationship mirrored a marriage, except I would not have to listen to these words: "Lisa, do you take such and such to be your lawful and wedded husband, to live together in marriage? Do you Lisa promise to love him, comfort him, honor and keep Him for better or worse, for richer or poorer, in sickness and health, forsaking all others? Be faithful only to him, for as long as you both shall live?" The expression on my face told the whole story, I had fallen into the trap of settling for less. I had to do an honest self-assessment. I had to confess that not once did I intentionally seek after sound matrimonial assistance prior to my making this life-altering decision. I also neglected to solicit counseling during those difficult periods in my marriages; steps I knew I would have taken for parenting advice or financial matters to avoid failing. Instead, I internalized my suffering, masked my pain and avoided the conversations that were difficult for me to face. I simply shut down this slice of my soul.

My mind was flooded with thoughts that I knew so little of the hard work it took to have a lifelong marriage. Previously, I assumed I understood the concept, because most of what I had been exposed to only revealed two options for a failing marriage: 1) you stay and suffer silently, or 2) you split. This was true for me until I sat still and did a little comparison shopping on all the relationships I valued. Something stuck out immediately: my responses in my marriage, my responses to my sons, and my responses to my friends were completely diverse. I noticed that I gave of myself easily and completely when it came to my children and my friends. Whether their actions warranted it or not, whether they told me they loved me or not, whether they made good choices or not, it was obvious even to the visually impaired that these types of responses were absent in my failed marriages. I didn't get the memo that explained how marriage works; that there will be trials and tribulations. I did not know that most days will be ordinary, mixed with hopeless moments and periodic extraordinary highs. I totally missed the memo that explained that, as times goes on, those same ordinary days I frequently complained about will mysteriously turn into blessing days because nothing unsolvable occurred. Those hopeless moment days are the ones I will be most thankful for because they produced the tests I will speak about in my testimonies. There was no memorandum sent out to make me aware that those unhappy moments that produce major amounts of tears will be used by God to build up my dependency on Him, or that as my godly character is manifested, I will have no problem serving my selfish nature its eviction notice and I will be grateful for the process. I saw no email message alerting me that the extraordinary highlights that resemble those in romantic movies, love songs and romance novels don't happen every day. No emphasis was given as to how I must plan to cling to my spouse during ordinary days, be intentional about our commitment to each other during the hopeless seasons, and remain humble during the highlight periods. No certified mail was sent explaining how, in the aftermath of tragic events, if we forge together, unbreakable bonds will be created that connect us forever, if we wait it out without complaining. No overnight package arrived expressing that how we handle real life situations will be the fabric that keeps us bonded together.

It never crossed my mind to craft a list of required topics in which dialogue could be generated to get answers to questions I'm sure needed to be answered prior to my saying I do. Circling around my brain right now are some obvious questions I should have contemplated, such as, are we remotely compatible? What type of character does this individual exhibit that I'm so willing to spend the rest of life discovering? Do we even possess the necessary skills needed to be married or, in other words, are we even the slightest bit competent enough to be married? Do we effectively communicate with each other regarding uncomfortable subjects, or do we just shut down when we feel as if we are not being heard or afraid? Do we have solutions for these types of responses? If not, are we willing to seek them together? How do we feel about the children that we will share in this union? How do we handle money and our financial obligations? Are we both willing to give each other access to our credit reports prior to walking down the aisle? Are we proactive about health matters? Do we both know how to exercise self-restraint when needed? What are the plans for retirement? What are our habits concerning cooking and cleaning? Do we make each other laugh? Are we willing to be vulnerable at the expense of possibly being rejected or looking foolish? I know it sounds simple, but trust me; it is the undiscussed topics that have the potential power to damage or ruin any relationship.

I am reminded how extremely important it is to get to know the person you plan to spend the rest of your life with. Use the dating period to sightsee and learn about your potential partner prior to making the serious marriage commitment. Use your time together wisely to explore and discover each other's likes and dislikes. Be truthful and ask yourself whether, if certain things don't change, can you live with those things forever. Discover who they are authentically and ask uncomfortable questions, like "Is there something about that person that brings out a part of me no one else gets to see?" If you are thinking it, deal with it. Men are not moved emotionally as women are although, depending on the subject, they can be just as sensitive. Observe how they interact in other relationships they consider important. See if their actions and their heart is pleasing towards the things of God. If you are paying attention with your spiritual eyesight, it will not take you long to figure out whether they are a counterfeit. It's difficult to maintain godly habits on a long-term basis if it's not your natural way of being. Without godly character traits, it is far too much work and stress to maintain a successful marriage. However, if that person is genuine, you will be able to tell if their motives are pure. Please don't believe the hype that your significant other should know what you require, desire, love, lack or are afraid of just because you have been hanging out together for a while. We are all different, we come from different backgrounds and receive information differently, so own your part in the relationship. If you are unable to convey your message, the problem may not necessarily be the other person. It could be because your communication skills are limited. When in doubt lean on your community and your circle of family and friends for guidance. They generally can see what you refuse to see, because they are not blinded by love.

By my early forties I finally got the truth about marriage. I understood that it is so much more than exclusive dating. It is a covenant between God and an imperfect man and woman who desire to commit to each other for a lifelong journey. It is the definitive vow of loyalty, responsibility and allegiance. It's funny how now that I am single and divorced, I'm asking God about marriage. Talk about backwards; if I only should have, could have. The uncovering of how important marriage is to God discloses how when biblically entered, God's original intent for marriage did not include divorce. Divorce was only introduced because of the hardening of man's heart, but God still desires for us to remain faithful in our marriages. It is clear from my actions that my heart was completely hardened. I was so self-focused, and my head was so completely buried deep in the sand that I let denial, pride, the blame game, unreasonable expectations, anger and a faithless victim mentality kick me out of the game. God's desire is always for us to establish godly, healthy, committed, loving productive relationships that unbelievers would want to replicate, just like salvation. They would recognize that marriage is the place where you are willing to publicly declare that for the rest of your life you vow to be accountable, responsible, and to submit your authority to another person with God as your foundation. In other words, you are proclaiming that you will entrust all that you currently are as well as all that you will ever be in the future to the care of this one individual. You openly announce that you are willing to walk through life with this person no matter what opposition enters your pathway. You must be willing to do whatever it takes to ensure that you stay together, in the utmost level of dedication and devotion.

It's taken a while, but I can admit that I never implemented this process in any of my previous relationships. Well, it is better late than never. Since I am no longer in conflict with myself, being a hostage to my past has ceased. Instead I redirected my energy into discovering the power of living in the now. Yes, I did contribute to my previous destructive life because of my ignorance of not knowing my identity or worth. I couldn't relate or accept for myself what God was voicing to me through Jeremiah 29:11 Amplified Bible (AMP). "For I know the plans and thoughts that I have for you, says the LORD, plans for peace and well-being and not for disaster, to give you a future and a hope." I was so twisted on the inside, it was easier for me to accept the deception of my former actions as truth that to cleave to what God's word reveals in Psalm 139:14 Amplified Bible (AMP). "I will give thanks and praise to You, for I am fearfully and wonderfully made."

Fast forward to present day life. I am extremely grateful that after my fifty-plus years on earth I have matured from a high-strung, feisty, bubbly young lady to a destiny-driven, faithful, trustworthy woman who doesn't run and hide when she sees her reflection in the mirror. Instead, she embraces every flaw, every scar, every emotion steering back at her, because they confirm she is more than a conqueror.

I have come to realize how my reckless attitude as a young adult, who thought I had all the answers, caused me to stumble. Please take note: we must never think too highly of ourselves. I have come to understand that all my inappropriate thoughts and actions were directly connected to the pain I underwent and ignored. The fact that I felt undervalued and unappreciated thrust me into self-sabotaging mode. Because of my unwillingness to be completely honest with myself, my initial attempts at counseling were unproductive. The results were less than positive in the beginning. I froze when it came time for me to be real, and I allowed my representative to show up during the pre-contemplation stage. I had no intention of changing; my objective for counseling was artificial. I wasn't looking to fix myself; I was looking for assistance to fix my spouse, who by the way was not even in the room. It was my safeguard move to protect the authentic Lisa, who was buried so deep within she was unrecognizable to anyone other than God. It was during the contemplation stage that I became open to receiving information and more willing to consider the possible consequences of my behavior, because my methods were not working. For a marriage to thrive once it loses its way, creating stacks of barriers as protection is not the solution. It was here I struggled with myself the most. It was difficult for me to understand why I was able to achieve success at being a parent and in my career, but I was a complete failure at marriage. The disappointment landed me in unfamiliar territory where I had no clue how to recover or to salvage what was missing. So, like an insane addict, I kept repeating the same actions, hoping for a different result. In the back of my mind, I knew my approach was not beneficial. What I discovered is that one can only receive useful, applicable instructions from those in authority, when you permit the authentic person to show up to the therapy appointments. There had to be a shift in my behavior. I had to be willing to open my wounded heart to receive what life has to offer, even when my circumstances had no observable change. By the time I arrived at the preparation stage of therapy, it was only the authentic Lisa and the therapist in the room. During this stage, I put my focus on me and used counseling to provide me with the support and direction I needed to truly live through the most **difficult** times of my life. By the time I arrived at the action stage, where real change occurs. I had no problem making the decision to move forward and I started planning and preparing for the changes I contemplated. I was no longer in crisis mode. My identity was secure because it could only be found in Jesus. The last stage of therapy - maintenance - can be the most challenging because we tend to become complacent once our goals have been met. I had to be very mindful of this phase because I did not want the old, familiar ways of coping to resurface. Maintenance is now a part of my quarterly life review.

By doing the work, I am now prepared and available for marriage if by chance it is presented. I already know my God is an equal opportunity God. My close relationship with God has prepared me for the level of intimacy required to be a godly wife. The romantic movies, love songs and romance novels that I have described to my friends as the type of marriage I desired are no longer the pre-requisite. The aspiration has shifted to a love experience with someone who is willing to lay down their life for me - not just someone who is eager to lay down *with* me. There is a difference. Clarifying my needs has stopped me from romanticizing about marriage to intentional living. What I am in search of is a marriage whose foundation rests solely on the shoulders of God; a relationship that is built upon a godly friendship, where we both are willing to put the needs of each other ahead of our own. A relationship where effective communication is evident, compromise is not a foreign, action and we understand that not all battles require us to fight; that prayer is sufficient. Someone who cares enough to know my brokenness, anticipates my fears, and is still committed to our merger that I would be willing to reciprocate. A relationship where we are both committed to enjoying the twists and turns of life together. A marriage where we both freely breathe apart and together that lasts a life time. The immature undeveloped philosophy I had towards marriage fortunately has been rehabilitated. Now I know all things are possible for me when I'm aligned with God.

Acknowledgements

Writing a book is harder than I thought and more rewarding than I could have ever imagined. Thank you, God, for entrusting me with such an awesome vision. Thank you, Jesus for being the only gateway for me to receive the Jeremiah 29:11 life I so desired. Thank you, Holy Spirit for guiding me through this process.

I am eternally grateful to my sons: Chris and Devin, who encouraged me to follow my dreams. Although my life has been filled with countless ups and downs, my journey is worth it. To my dad, James, my mom Renee, my sister Latina and my deceased brother James Jr., aka Dino, without our experiences, your love and support there would be no "Dangerously Different" book to share.

My circle of friends, Carla, Calvin, Darlene, Yolanda, Missie Dawn, Andrea, Betty, Donnetta, Tammy, India and Kelly, what can I say, we are all different, yet what is common is my authentic love for each of you. Thank you for always encouraging me, loving me, praying for me, supporting me and listening to my outbursts of what I am going to do next, especially during the planning stages.

Complete thanks to everyone at WestBow Press whose enthusiastic support, great advice and insightful feedback helped to polish my efforts. I am forever indebted to Wendy at Blue Note Writing for her editorial help, keen insight, and ongoing support in bringing my book to life.

I want to thank EVERYONE who has ever crossed my path and taught me something healthy and positive about love. I heard you, and it meant the world to me.

Love You Real Hard!

Printed in the United States
By Bookmasters